Juggling

OR: HOW TO BE A JUGGLER

Rupert Ingalese
With annotations by Thom Wall

Modern Vaudeville Press
PHIADELPHIA, PENNSYLVANIA

Copyright © 2019 by Rupert Ingalese & Thom Wall.

All rights reserved. No part of this publication may be reproduced, distributed or transmitted in any form or by any means, including photocopying, recording, or other electronic or mechanical methods, without the prior written permission of the publisher, except in the case of brief quotations embodied in critical reviews and certain other noncommercial uses permitted by copyright law. For permission requests, write to the publisher, addressed "Attention: Permissions Coordinator," at the address below.

Modern Vaudeville Press
113 E. Mayland St
Philadelphia, PA 19144, USA
www.modernvaudevillepress.com

Ordering Information:
Quantity sales. Special discounts are available on quantity purchases by corporations, associations, and others. For details, contact the "Special Sales Department" at the address above.

Juggling / Rupert Ingalese
ISBN 978-1-7339712-0-1

CONTENTS

What is this Book?   1

Introduction   5

How and Where to Practise   13

Ball Juggling   15

Preliminary Practice   20

Feats of Balancing   33

Juggling with Plates   38

Juggling with Bottles   45

A Few Hints on Juggling with Clubs   49

Tricks with Hats, Umbrellas, Etc.   55

Addendum   72

Acknowledgements   85

Other Titles by Modern Vaudeville Press   86

Free eBook!   90

Juggling

∴

BY
RUPERT INGALESE

∴

1921

FOR PRICE LIST OF HIGH-CLASS JUGGLING GOODS

As supplied to the Profession

SEE BACK PAGES.

There is nothing new except what has been forgotten.

- French proverb

What is this Book?

RUPERT INGALESE, BORN PAUL Wingrave, was a British juggler who worked in the first half of the 1900s, both as a juggler and as a producer and manager of variety shows across England.

Ingalese's performances, as we know by searching through online newspaper databases, were very well recieved. The first review to appear of his work was printed on September 14th, 1920, in *The Daily Mail*:

The variety programme at the Tivoli this week is of high standard. At the top of the bill is Rupert Ingalese and his flunkeys, supported by Miss Angela Grey (pianist). Rupert Ingalese proves himself a skillful juggler and performs with one hand whilst he plays the piano with the other.

On May 31st, 1921, *The Daily Telegraph* called him "...a juggler of bewildering skill and finesse."

A few years later, on March 18th, 1924, *The Citizen* called Ingalese's performance in a top-notch musical variety show "...one of the best things in the programme."

Ingalese wasn't the only remarkable act in the shows he produced. *The Devon and Exeter Gazette* offered the following remarks about his production *A Show Superlative* on July 29th, 1930:

A Show Superlative, which opened to good houses at Exeter Hippodrome last night, claims to be the pioneer road show - but it woul dbe a great mistake to suppose that it contains a single back number. It is a very successful effort to please everybody, for while one moment one is admiring equilibristic feats, the next moment brings the sheer loveliness of classical music - and then we are left laughing by some delicious fooling....

...it is impossible to assign precedence to any turn when ability was expressed in such diverse ways. The Auklands gave some excellent concertina playing, but one of the most impressive moments in their turn was when the "house" sat hushed, listening to "Little Tweet," their canary, singing as though his little throat would burst.

Another small (but not quite so dimumitive) performer was Wee Teddy. This boy - he cannot be much more than twelve - kept the audience entertained by a sole turn to such effect that he had to decline an encore, pointing out that he was to reappear later in the programme.

Two things contributed to the popularity of Grifi the clown. He blew bubbles of such elasticity and strength that considerable liberties could be taken with them. And he offered to give a free morning or afternoon performance to any hospital or institution in Exeter. It is to be hoped that this generous offer will be accepted.

The famous Russian Bayan Singers do not speak English, but gave delight through the universal language of good music. Their renderings included the "Barcarole" from "Tales of Hofmann," a marvellous vocal blend. Warroner seemed undecided whether to let comedy or his skill as a violinist predominate. He was a whimsical soul, but his technique, both in staccato and harmonics, was faultless...

...Rupert Ingalese, assisted with his gorgeously apparelled flunkeys, juggled with much of the contents of a drawing room, adding the maniuplation of flaming torches to his finale.

Cyril Johnson rode a bicycle forwards, backwards, and at remarkable angles, at one time carrying his several accomplished lady assistants as a crew. Enough has been said to indicate the ingredients of an evening's good entertainment.

Ingalese's career continued into the late 1930s - he continued to both produce shows and perform a staple act. His hometown paper, the *Exeter and Plymouth Gazette* published the following report of his tricks on October 19, 1937:

[Ingalese] is no stranger to Exeter, and for about a quarter of an hour again delights with his quick juggling entertainment, into which he has introduced new and effective work. A steady hand and a keen eye are essential to successful juggling, and Rupert Ingalese must possess these or he would be unable to do many of his tricks. His juggling with money is a small but difficult feat, and this is interlarded with other work, some of which require much care. Heavy articles and delicate things, like eggs and glass, are balanced on poles, precariously placed on head or face. Most of us find it none too easy to do one job effectively at once; Rupert Ingalese shows us how to do six at one time, and do one and all well. His act is artistically staged and efficiently presented.

Also performing in this particular show were The Moxham Trio of "cycling fools"; Gene Morelle, a musician who played bicycle pumps, bellows, car tires, and other other non-instruments (and whose impression of a train leaving the station and disappearing into the distance apparently brought the house down); Connie Grahame and Hal Scott, who sang, danced, and contorted their faces; the singer and trick-whistler Gladys Church; Ernie Whitmee, a nonogenerian comedian who sings about his age; an octette of acrobatic dancers named The Hoffman Lovelies; and Clifton and Young, a man and woman comedy duo who "indulge in much comedy play and patter."[1]

And, on top of these accolades, Rupert also wrote a book.

If his performances were so consistently successful and his troupe so in demand, why did he write this text? Was this a springboard for his career? Was he trying to cash in on his fame? Was this an attempt to selflessly spread the joy of juggling, some 26 years before the International Jugglers' Association would be founded? The answers to these questions are lost in time as Ingalese passed long ago. We are left with one fact, however - the book is quality.

Your humble team at Modern Vaudeville Press is delighted to re-release this public domain work along with a number of annotations by Thom Wall, a juggler and researcher who specializes in juggling techniques from the turn of the century - who (thankfully) is not dead quite yet.

---

1   If you agree that this sounds like an incredible show, your humble editor commends your good taste.

Introduction

WHEN I WAS A very young child, playing in the street in the little Yorkshire town where I was born, there came along the pavement a being clad it seemed to me, in nothing but an overcoat and slippers. Closer observation, however, revealed the fact that his flesh was covered with a thin stuff of some sort, nearly the colour of his skin, and clinging as closely to it.

After the first feeling of surprise at the sight of him, I next wondered how he had got into such a tight-fitting costume, and I believe I concluded he must have been boiled and poured into it! Little except his neck and the lower parts of his limbs was visible, and a broad bright ribbon encircled his head to keep close his long, coal-black hair. Naturally I joined the little crowd that was following in his wake, with wonder and delight. He presently came to a stop; and, dropping to the ground a half-filled sack he had been carrying, took therefrom a piece of carpet. This he spread upon the roadside, and emptied on to it the contents of the bag - consisting of glittering balls, metal rings and knives. He then, with a dramatic air, threw off his overcoat and stood revealed to my astonished and admiring gaze - a JUGGLER, in all the glory of tights and spangles.[2] He produced a triangular-shaped article (which I after-

---

[2] This passage reminds your editor of the following lines from Ganthan Roberts' *Bunkum Entertainments*, an 1895 text for boys on how to pretend to do juggling feats: "The juggling should be done in evening dress, when it must be announced as an imitation of a juggler, or done without announcement in the costume of a street tumbler, which should be grotesque if not verging on the outrageous. The kissing of hands and bowing with the hand on heart must be induced in after each swindle, as though great dexterity has been exhibited."

wards knew as Pan's pipes), and this he thrust into a receptacle slung beneath his chin. Then taking up a drum which had formed part of his impedimenta, he opened the performance with a loud and brilliant flourish. And such music! A carping critic might have complained that like Clonglocketty's air on the Bagpipes:

"It was wild, it was fitful, as wild as the breeze,
"It wandered about into several keys:"

...but to my enraptured ears it was the sweetest melody, and told, like the music of the Pied Piper to the children of Hamelin, of

"A joyous land . . .
"Where waters gushed and fruit trees grew,
"And flowers put forth a fairer hue,
"And everything was strange and new."

I have heard good music since then, but nothing that has ever thrilled me like that stirring overture.

The impression made upon my mind by this "Solomon in all his Glory," and his wondrous performance, has hardly faded yet. The man was only of medium height, but his bull-neck, his broad chest and muscles bulging like pictures I had seen of Roman gladiators, his dark defiant eye and his general air, conveyed the impression (to me at all events) of gigantic strength. All that followed was like a beautiful dream: a blissful vision of a form clothed in gorgeous raiment, walking or standing amid a shower of glistening balls and gleaming knives. The dream was brought to a close by finding the performer standing beside me, cap in hand, begging coppers from the bystanders. It seemed monstrous that such a thing could be, but I postponed consideration of the matter. Darting from the crowd I made all speed home, some distance away; and, obtaining what few pence my passionate entreaties could extort from my parents, I hurried back to find my Juggler gone. I ran up and down every street in the town to find him. Marvel to me it was that none of my playmates seemed to have heard of or seen him. He had indeed "gone from my gaze" as effectually as if the earth had opened and swallowed him, or as if he had ascended into the clouds, from whence belike he had descended. I never saw my Juggler more, though I sought hard for him in after years. Watching him as a child on that never-to-be-forgotten afternoon, I was blind to what was visible enough to my mind's eye in later years.

As the reader will see, the man had made an extraordinary impression on my childish imagination. I should have dearly loved to have met him again, and would have given much for the chance. Apart from the mere interest and pleasure it would have afforded me to have seen him go through his performance once again, a strong feeling of pity moved me. As I have said, things became clear with later experience that the child was incapable of discerning. The lines on his once handsome face told of hardship, suffering, and bitter disappointment. I have heard through all these intervening years the racking cough that shook his well-knit frame, and which he tried in vain to stifle. The poor fellow is probably gathered to his fathers ere this, and

"Sleeps in the vault where all the Capulets do lie."
Peace to his ashes! May he rest in peace.

But if my Divinity had departed, he had left his influence behind him. "The heart of a Juggler was made that day." To become a Strolling Performer, clad in that resplendent and bespangled garb, wandering through green and shady lanes, emerging into towns and villages, to dazzle the eyes of crowds with my showy dress: to hear their out-spoken admiration of my powerful form and feats of strength, their murmurs of horror as the murderous-looking knives whirled gleaming through the air, and their loud cheers at its close: to be all this, to live all this, was to my conception the very acme of felicity, human or divine. Indeed it seemed doubtful at times if one could attain to such a height of bliss and live.

This fascination for the life of a strolling acrobat (or Juggler), kept full possession of my mind till I was well into my 'teens. But I have to admit that there were times when it had occurred to me that there might be some vicissitudes even in such an exalted spheres. The poor acrobat's far-off look of mingled sorrow, disappointment and resignation haunted me.[3] But about this time I chanced to be taken to an entertainment in a large town near which we lived. Here to my inexpressible delight a "turn" was done by a high-class Juggler. It was Charlene; in my opinion, the finest Juggler of that time, and of whom I shall make further mention later.

If doubts had occasionally possessed my mind as to my choice of a profession, they disappeared now. I had not seen or heard of any Juggler but the one I have described: not had I ever pictured one in my imagination different from the hero of my childhood's days, with his fleshings, gaudy head-gear, spangles, pipes and drum. Now another and very different picture was presented to my view. The scene had changed from a village street to the well-appointed stage of a high-class Music Hall, with its beautiful scenery, festooned curtains, dazzling foot-lights and all the other appurtenances of a modern proscenium. Amid a flourish of music from the skilled orchestra, a man of splendid presence scarcely past his youth stopped on to the stage, and with a graceful salute to his cheering audience began his turn. The several parts of his entertainment were accompanied with appropriate music by the band, and were gone through with an ability, case and grace that fascinated the beholders, and at the

---

3   The professional circus artists reading this book are doubtlessly nodding in agreement.

close of his clever performance the loud and continued plaudits testified to the delight of the large assembly.

I fear my readers will have begun to think this more of a gossipy sort of autobiography than a practical treatise on "How to become a Juggler": but I must tell them of a dream that swept to the winds any remaining doubt or hesitation as to my choice of a profession.

Though little more than a schoolboy, I had already begun to think it was about time I decided upon my future career.

One day, I was wandering among the hayfields of the country side,

"'Twas in June,
"One of June's brightest days, the bee, the bird,
"The butterfly were on their brightest wing."

In an adjoining field, a group of men and women were at work, and the breeze wafted the sound of their merry laughter and the scent of the new-mown hay across the road. With a hay-cock for a pillow, I laid me down, and presently was fast asleep.

I found myself a stronger wandering aimlessly up and down the streets of a large town, and from the posters flaring from every available spot I learned that the great Señor Caravanalli was coming that night. Who Señor Caravanalli was, or why he was great, I had not the faintest idea. I remembered that his high-sounding foreign name was very similar to one I had ambitiously decided to adopt as my stage name if I ever faced the foot-lights. I felt no real interest in the poster's announcement however. Approaching nearer the centre of the town, the faint air of expectancy, which had but slightly permeated its suburbs, increased to an extraordinary degree. Cabs and broughams, private motors and taxis filled with bejewelled ladies, and gentlemen in evening dress, were dashing through the streets. A long queue of people stretched far up the pavement and round a corner: police officers were at every few yards to keep the sidewalk clear, while above, below, to right and left and in front, the great man's name filled the air. I wandered on to where the interest seemed converging. Here the scene was the most animated I had ever beheld. It was a magnificent square, brilliantly illuminated. In the centre stood the Hall, an imposing building with lofty pillars, and literally a blaze of light; while from every part of the Hall and Square, in every device that fancy or ingenuity could suggest, in initial, cypher, and monogram, in gas, electricity, or Chinese lantern, was worked the magic name. A glittering bayonet or gleam of scarlet uniform here and there, told that royalty was honouring the occasion with its presence. My interest was now thoroughly aroused. Who and what could be this high and mighty Señor Caravanalli, whose visit created such a furore of curiosity and excitement? In my dream I was a grown man and had never heard his name. I asked, or rather attempted to ask, for information; but met with a similar experience to that of the Yankee at the Court of King Arthur.

A very few informed me that Señor Caravanalli was coming but when I asked who he was, I only received a look of pity or contempt for my ignorance. A sudden and violent commotion amongst the crowd showed me the doors had been flung open, and I found myself borne along by the surging mass of humanity into the immense building. The place was packed from floor to ceiling. Not only was every inch of standing room occupied, but the audience seemed hanging from the front of the galleries, and even from the very pillars, like swarming bees. The buzz was instantly hushed as the orchestra struck up the opening bars of a beautiful overture. Then the music was changed to a lively prelude foretelling the great man's advent. This evoked such a roar of greeting and applause that assuredly it might have been heard a mile away. In the midst of it Señor Caravanalli appeared on the stage.

Never in my life, neither in my dreams nor when awake, have I felt such a sense of surprise and perplexity as I experienced that night. From my coign of vantage, (a front seat in the lower gallery, opposite the stage and its occupant) I had an unimpeded view. Now I noticed, what I had not seen when the curtain was rung up, all the adjuncts of the modern Juggler tastefully displayed about the stage. At sight of the bowing figure, I felt myself giving vent to a cry of bewilderment. Was I mad? No! surely not, only dreaming. I strove, as I have never striven before or since, to wake myself. I wrenched myself round and looked for some time at the sea of faces behind me, I rubbed my eyes and tried hard to smile at my idiotic, maddening, fancy. Then I looked again. I could doubt no longer. The great Señor Caravanalli was - MYSELF.

The performance was over. There was a rush to see the "star" drive off - which he did in a pair-horse brougham, amid a shower of bouquets and cheers. And I awoke!

My readers will have gathered that my determination to become a Juggler had strengthened with my growth, and when I left school I gave all my spare time to learning and practising the art. But I found it terribly slow work and I made but little progress. I could find no books dealing with the subject. Works on Ventriloquism, Conjuring and other pastimes were to be had; but, as far as I could ascertain, no treatise affording instruction to the aspirant in Juggling had ever been published.[4]

Now these pages, a record of my own personal experience, have been written with the view of affording help, and practical information, to those who aspire to become expert in the fascinating science. Conjuring and Juggling are often confounded with each other, but they

---

4   Endearing as this sentiment is, there were indeed juggling manuals in existance at the time (though likely not in a public library accessible to young Ingalese!) Stanyon's *Magic Magazine*, for example, was published from 1900 through 1920 and frequently contained short lessons on juggling technique.

have little in common.⁵ Juggling is skill, my Masters: Conjuring is trickery. Any intelligent person with a few pounds to spend in "properties," and sufficient interest in the diversion, may become a fairly proficient Conjuror in a comparatively short space of time. Not so with the subject of this little work. Juggling is a science requiring not only interest and perseverance on the part of the scholar but proper instruction for its acquirement. Moreover, the steady practice necessary is greatly calculated to develop those admirable qualities of the mind, patience and diligence: and few pastimes are better adapted to improve the general physique, every muscle of the body being brought into constant action.

---

5   This conflation was even more common in Ingalese's time than it is our own. Ingalese himself was referred to as magician in a few newspaper articles, including the February 10, 1923 edition of *Brooklyn Life,* which called him England's "master magician."

In fact, the word "juggling" was first used in 1897 to refer to the skill of throwing and catching obtained by practice that is familiar with our modern English speakers. However, the practice of juggling (in our modern understanding of it) was often lumped in with magicians and a host of other variety acts in this time. Ingalese writes this book around the same time that Enrico Rastelli and other "pure" jugglers worked on stage - the very first entertainers who were billed whole-heartedly for their prowess in throwing and catching. For more on these linguistic complexities, refer to the final chapter of *Juggling - From Antiquity to the Middle Ages,* by Modern Vaudeville Press.

How and Where to Practise

BEFORE ENTERING ON OUR course of instruction it will be as well to give a few hints as to how and where to practise. Plenty of space is necessary - especially height; and, needless to say, plenty of light is quite as important. I would recommend those of my readers who seriously intend going in for Juggling to join a gymnasium. It is an ideal place for practising, with all the advantages of space and light, loftiness and, last not least, gymnasium mats. Whether practising with balls, plates, or clubs, or doing "heavy" Juggling with such "properties" as cannon-balls, etc., these mats will be found of great utility both in breaking their fall and stopping their roll. During practice, of course, they are continually dropping and rolling about. The mats should be placed so as to form a square immediately in front of the place where you intend to stand. It is best to be a short distance away from the edge of the mats: say, ten to twelve inches. If you stand too close you are liable to trip over then while reaching out for anything, you may have thrown a little beyond your reach. When practising balancing tricks it is best not to use the mats at all, as you require sufficient clear floor space to allow you to move about in order to retain the equilibrium of the article balanced.

Of course, daylight is the best for all these exercises, and the light should be at your back so that your eyes may not encounter a glare when you turn them in any particular direction.[6] Windows, if in front or nearly so, should have the blinds drawn. A dark foreground with a good light from behind is preferable. The same rule holds good in regard to artificial light. Practise with all the lights behind you when it is possible. When it is not, shade any lamps that must be in front of you.

---

6   Your humble editor agrees in principle with this statement but would like to remind readers that when juggling for a living, they won't always have control over the lights. While it can be helpful to practice in perfect conditions, unless you can execute a trick with a glare in your eyes, you may not be ready for stage!

Ball Juggling

SUPPOSE WE BEGIN WITH perhaps the most popular, and very showy feats: namely, the various kinds of Ball Juggling. Though to some extent out of fashion with modern Jugglers, this is as necessary to a Juggler's education as scale practice to the scholar in music. We have some wonderful manipulators of the flying balls still with us. Amongst the foremost of these is Pierre Amoros, who juggled with nine billiard balls and who now, I believe, performs the unprecedented feat of keeping ten balls in the air.[7] There is also Rapoli who "showers" five balls in a

---

[7] Legend says that Amoros' prowess with nine-ball juggling was what prompted Rastelli to learn ten! Amoros toured as part of the "Werner and Amoros Company." The *Hartford Courant* gives the following report on their performance on April 7, 1914: "The real headliner, from a popular standpoint, is the offering of the Werner and Amoros Company. This company of four present a number of original and difficult juggling stunts, their finest work being done with a large number of plates that fly from one end of the stage to the other with wonderful rapidity. The closing feature of the act is entirely different, taking the form of a high-class musical act, with the rendition of tuneful music on a piano, a violin, and a cello. There is a surprise in the finale that is not looked for." By the 1920s, the company seems to have shed its fourth member and continued touring, often billed as "jugglers and comedians" who presented novel feats. (Per the *San Francisco Chronicle*, June 13, 1920).

right-hand direction, and then without a stop or pause, reverses, and "showers" them in a left-hand direction.[8] Charlene is another famous performer who executes feats with seven or eight balls as easily as many jugglers would with four or five.[9] Of course these performances are without parallel in the profession, and are the result of the study and persevering practice of a lifetime. But those of my readers who steadily and pluckily keep up their practice will reap the reward due to diligence, and will soon acquire a degree of dexterity which will render easy the accomplishment of more and more difficult feats.

First, as to the best class of ball. Some artistes use billiard-balls, others tennis-balls, whilst a few prefer metal balls.[10] My objections to all the foregoing are, that billiard-balls are too heavy - especially when manipulating five or more. They are very apt to clash with one another, and fly off at a tangent with great force; at considerable risk of damage

---

8   Not much is known about Rapoli, save for a handful of newspaper articles. *The Democrat and Chronicle* describes Rapoli's act on July 27, 1914, as such: "Rapoli, juggler of chariot wheels, cannon balls and projectiles... considered a wonder by those who know of his work. Two comedians assist him, and it is said that they provoke laughter of the spontaneous kind." Karl-Heinz Ziethen notes in *Juggling - The Past and Future* that Rapoli was a top-class ball juggler who performed up to eight balls.

9   According to Karl-Heinz Ziethen, Charlene performed a musical juggling act called "Charlene & Charlene." *The Guardian* wrote about Charlene's performance on November 17, 1908, reporting that Charlene would "[come] into a drawing room and desperately [juggle], and when he is tired, Charlene (a lady) arrives and xylophones... [producing] a tripping, tinny melody." In their November 4, 1970 retrospective, *Punch* magazine reports that Charlene & Charlene would also juggle and play the violin simultaneously.

10   This statement is a sign of Ingalese's times. This book was written before there was such a thing as a mass-produced juggling ball. The invention of plastics, mass-production, and injection-molding happened long after this book was originally written. So, in this time, jugglers were relegated to finding appropriate materials that were not necessarily manufactured for the purposes of stage performance. Though this warrants an annotation today, in the past this would have been as mundane a statement as "some jugglers like using bean-bags, others prefer stage balls. Others still use russians - hollow balls half-filled with sand."

to the tyro[11] practising, and to anything breakable they may encounter in their wild flight. Furthermore, if the performer perspires much, the smooth ivory surface becomes damp and slippery much sooner than any other. Tennis-balls are too large and too light (when juggling more than four), while metallic ones have practically the same disadvantages as billiard balls. The kind my experience has led me to adopt as most suitable are balls of hard rubber, slightly smaller than a full-sized billiard-ball. These are about the right weight and are very satisfactory in every way, as they do not get damaged or out of shape, and do not get slippery in the hand. They may be bought at most of the toyshops and sports-outfitters, for a few coppers each.[12] Let me remind the budding Juggler that it is well to accustom himself to use always one kind of ball. He will find it a great loss of practice (as well as costly) if, after becoming somewhat expert with one particular size and weight, he discards it for another kind of a different size or a different weight.

And now, having procured a number of balls of the right kind, let us proceed to see what we can do with them.

There are several different styles of Ball Juggling for two hands. The three most used are:

---

11   Though it's pretty to think that the word tyro is a playful take on a romance language's verb for "to throw" (for example, Spanish - *tirar*, Italian - *tirare*), this word is a departure from Medieval Latin's *tiro* meaning "a young recruit."

12   The very first set of mass-produced juggling balls were this style - hard rubber, and smaller than a billiard ball. They were made by Harry Moll of Denver, Colorado, in 1949 and were sold in boxed sets of six with the phrase "Now you can learn juggling" merrily drawn on the box's lid. These sets can frequently be found on sites like eBay today.

(1) Cascading, or throwing the balls into the air from one hand to another, performing the same movement with the left hand as with the right, so that the balls pass and re-pass in the centre. See fig. 1.

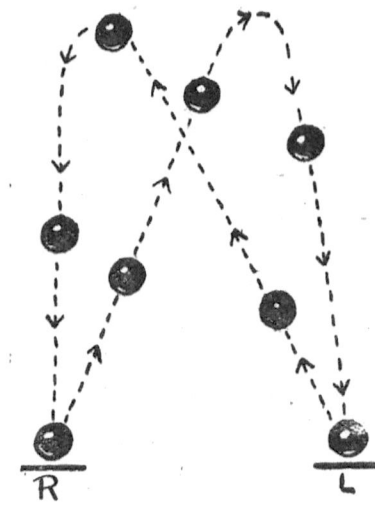

"CASCADE"
FIG. 1.

(2) Showering, or throwing the balls from hand to hand, so as to produce the appearance of a circular or oval figure. See Fig. 2.

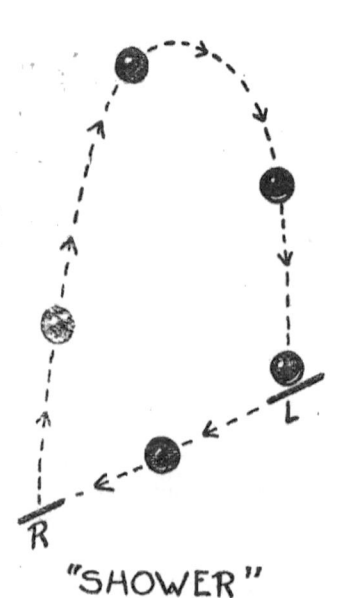

"SHOWER"
FIG. 2.

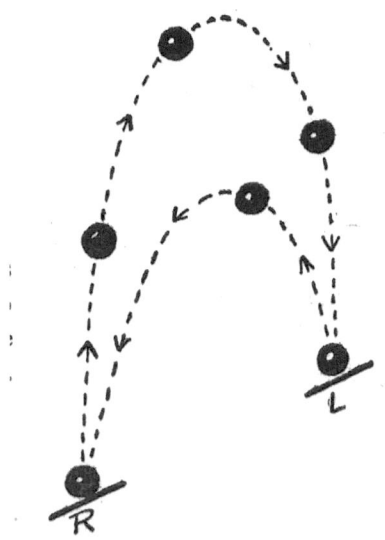

(3) Double Showering, or throwing the balls from hand to hand, so as to form a double-looped figure—one loop inside the other. See Fig. 3.[13]

"DOUBLE SHOWER"
FIG. 3.

None of these feats are exactly easy, of course. There would be many more competent Jugglers in this world, if they were: but they can all be accomplished by anyone who is determined to succeed, who will give the time and patience necessary for practising, and who goes about it in the right way.

So, before I describe in detail how to do the Cascade and the Showers, I will describe the preliminary practice which is necessary to every style of Ball Juggling.

---

13   The "double shower" is known as the "half shower" today.

Preliminary Practice

THE FIRST THING TO be done is to practise throwing one ball to varying heights, and learning to catch it again neatly and gracefully-and with certainty-in every conceivable position.

One-Ball Practice - Practising with one ball will not be found very entertaining to the beginner, but it will make very much easier the work which is to come and lay a good foundation for other styles of Juggling. Throw the ball up from the right hand to heights varying between one and six or seven feet. This should be persevered in until the ball can be thrown and caught with the right hand with but little effort. Throw the ball as nearly vertical as possible so that it comes down to the place whence it started: thereby obviating unnecessary reaching out for it.[14] A Juggler, in all his public performances should keep his feet as still as possible, and move from his original "stance" only when it is absolutely necessary to the performance of a particular feat. Practise the same movement with the left hand: then vary the procedure by throwing with the right and catching with the left: and, again, the other way about.

---

14 What's interesting here is that Ingalese does not talk about the hand-scoop that's taught as a part of modern juggling technique. Should a learner use this book and follow it to the letter, any attempt at a four-ball fountain (or similar pattern) would be hindered by collisions, as the author insists that the balls travel through the same trajectory above the hand on both ascent and descent.

Now try throwing it up in front of you and catching it from under your leg. Next throw it up in front of you and catch it behind you; throw it up from behind you and catch it in front of you; throw it up and catch it in the many other ways you can devise for yourself as you progress. Lengthy and detailed instructions as to one-ball practice are obviously unnecessary, and would be an insult to the reader's intelligence.

Two-Ball Practice - The next thing to learn is to juggle two balls, first with the right hand, and then with the left. Take two balls in the right hand, throw one four or five feet high, and the moment it begins its descent throw up the other one in the same manner. Catch the descending one and return it into the air again, and so on. The balls in this practice are played with the right hand only. Repeat this throwing up and catching until it becomes quite easy. At the first few attempts this may be found a little difficult, but with half-an-hour's practice daily it will rapidly become mere child's play. A good plan is to count as each ball leaves the hand. Thus, if you can count up to ten, say, after a few days' practice, and up to fifteen after a few days more, you will be able definitely to estimate the progress you are making.[15] Then you must practise with the left hand until you are able to use it nearly as well as the right. I say nearly as well: because it is practically impossible for the majority of people to become absolutely ambidextrous. When able to juggle two balls in either hand you can attempt three. There are many different ways in which balls can be manipulated-particularly when only using three - but you will find none easier or afford better practice than the Cascade. The term "cascade" can really hardly be applied to a manipulation of only three balls, but is properly used to describe a movement with five or more.[16] You must begin with three, however, and

---

15   To your editor's knowledge, this is the first mention in English-language juggling literature of tracking your progress in a meaningful way. Other texts indicate that progress will take time, but none of them suggest measuring and recording your progress.

16   This is a curious assertion that modern jugglers would not

gradually increase the number as you become dexterous. You can't run until you have learnt to walk, you know.

To commence, take two balls in the right hand and one in the left. Lead off by throwing up one of the balls from the right hand, as you have already been taught; with a slightly inward motion, remembering that balls leaving one hand have to be caught by the other. Next the ball in the left hand should be thrown up (at the moment the first is about to descend) as nearly as possible to the same height in a slightly right-hand direction: the first ball thrown is now caught in the left hand, the second ball is in the air and the third ball is at once thrown up from the right hand in the same manner as the first. Playing three balls in this manner will soon be found very easy of accomplishment and should take very little time to learn.

Showering three balls is more difficult,[17] and the method should be first practised with two, as follows: take both balls in the right hand, and throw one from the right hand to the left; not straight across but with an upward and inward motion, making a sort of half circle from one-and-a-half to two feet high. The left hand receiving the ball must be about eighteen inches from the right and slightly higher. As soon as the first ball has left the right hand, send the other after it with an exactly similar throw: then catch the first ball in the left hand and immediately transfer it to the right by a short straight downward throw. Catch the

---

agree with - the term "cascade" is used today to refer to the base pattern with any odd-number of props.

17   From your humble editor's Western viewpoint and own practical experience, it's true that cascades are easier to juggle than showers. However, it should be noted that juggling in a "shower" pattern emerged in a number of cultures independently of the "cascade." Specifically, juggling games in the South Pacific, the Roman Empire, and various Native cultures across North America all juggled in a shower - not in a cascade. For more information about juggling patterns in ancient times, refer to *Juggling - From Antiquity to the Middle Ages* by Modern Vaudeville Press.

second ball and shoot it to the right hand: but, before it gets there, the first ball must have again started its journey to the left hand, and so on. This must be done over and over again till our future exponent of the Science has become expert in this particular movement. This he will do pretty quickly if he carefully follows the instructions given. The pupil will the more readily learn to Shower three or more balls by practising the above method with two balls than by commencing with three. I strongly advise him always to perfect himself in each part or movement he sets himself to learn, before proceeding to another. "Slow and sure" is old but excellent advice.

To Shower three balls, two are held in the right hand and one in the left. Precisely the same procedure must be followed as in showering two: with this important addition, that the first ball thrown should be sent up a little higher than the succeeding ones. This gives a little additional time to get the others after it. Immediately the first ball is away, send up the second after it; and quickly transfer the third from the left hand to the now empty right. As the first ball is caught in the left hand, the ball that has just been transferred to the right hand, must be at once thrown after the others as before.

I must here caution the learner not to throw the balls (or indeed any articles in other movements) too high; both because the longer time occupied in their passing through the air takes more judging, and because a great deal of effect is lost,[18] if balls are juggled too slowly as they must be if thrown too high. When proficiency has been attained in Cascading and Showering separately, a very pretty little movement may be practised, by Cascading with the three balls for a short time, and then

---

18   Here, we can see Ingalese's bias as a performer, rather than a pedagogue, in the advice he gives. Modern circus coaches generally advise students to embrace the height and learn to control the throw rather than relying on hand-speed to make a pattern work. Once control is established through practice, the pattern can be varied to achieve an effect.

passing into the Shower without stopping. This is an effective little trick. To I accomplish the above, commence Cascading and count each time a ball leaves the right hand, 1, 2, 3, up to, say, 12. After the twelfth has left the right hand, the next (viz., the thirteenth) must be thrown about as high again as the preceding ones, the fourteenth not quite so high. No. 12, which has now been caught in the left hand, must be quickly passed (as in Showering) to the right hand, where it becomes No. 15 and is quickly sent up after No. 14 (still as in Cascading). Now as the thirteenth reaches the left hand after its somewhat higher throw, shoot it to the right and proceed with the Shower, counting it No. 1. This is but one of the many simple, but showy, little changes that will suggest themselves to the devotee as he progresses in the art.[19]

To juggle three balls in one hand, the three should be held in the right hand and of course thrown up one after the other, each ball being made to take as nearly as possible the same line or direction as the preceding one. It might be thought that to play three balls with one hand they must be thrown to a great height. This is not so, seven or eight feet is sufficiently high for a beginner, who will find the higher he sends the balls the less control he has over them. They should not be thrown too quickly, but with deliberation, the third one leaving the hand as the first commences to descend.[20] The balls in this feat are apt to collide with each other a good deal in the earlier stages of practice, but patience and perseverance will overcome all difficulties, and success will be the reward. Of course, manipulating three balls with one hand is no child's exercise, and when our pupil can accomplish it easily and gracefully, he may regard himself as "coming on" in the science.

---

19   In Siteswap notation - the numerical system for recording juggling patterns developed some 60 years after this book was published - the transition Ingalese suggests here would be described as 51...7131...51

20   Modern jugglers would rightly scoff at this instruction - it's common knowledge today that the third ball is thrown when the first ball has already begun its descent downwards - when 2/3 of its total "flight path has been traveled."

In juggling four balls, the simplest method is to play two in each hand, (not passing them from one hand to another) as four being an even number, Cascading them, even to an expert Juggler is an awkward movement.[21] If fair proficiency has been acquired in playing two balls in each hand separately, not much practice will be found necessary to use the two hands at the same time with two balls in each. The awkward feeling first experienced in attempting to juggle with both hands at once, but working independently of each other, will soon pass off: and this will be found one of the easiest movements to acquire in ball-juggling. There are two ways of performing the foregoing: one is for the two hands and the four balls to keep time with each other, that is, throwing up a ball from each hand at the same second of time, and catching them simultaneously: and the other is to keep alternate time, throwing up a ball first with the right and then with the left and so on. The latter perhaps is a shade more difficult than the former. It is as well occasionally to lead off with the left, instead of the right hand, as tending to the acquirement of ambidexterity, but this remark does not apply to Showering.

Showering four balls is of course more advanced work, and will require considerably more practice than any of the foregoing. To commence Showering four the same instructions given for Showering three, holds good. I trust it is needless to say, that it is useless attempting this movement with four balls, until the tyro is expert in Showering three. Two balls are held in each hand: lead off with the right by throwing the first ball about two yards high, and quickly send up the other from the right hand: shoot one ball from the left hand to the right, and at once

---

21   A four-object cascade is - in the modern sense - an impossibility. There has been much discussion about what this might look like, and a few jugglers have made attempts at performing what this might look like (Mike Moore, Ameron Rosvall, et. al.) The pattern Ingalese is referring to here is likely 55550 or some other four-object pattern that maintains a cascade shape. A "true" four object cascade is not possible due to the restrictions within the language of siteswap.

send it up after the other two. The fourth ball is now transferred from left to right, and sent up in the wake of the others as the first ball is caught in the left hand. A month's hopeful, patient, intelligent practice should show good results. I will again remind my reader of the importance of holding the left hand a little higher than the right in Showering. I would also again advise him to pursue his study and practice of the science not only with all patience, but with cheerfulness and pleasure in his work.[22]

We are now about to deal with the more advanced stage of Ball-juggling - juggling with five balls or more. I must here point out that it is just as difficult, or impossible, to learn scientific juggling by simply reading instructions in black and white and not practising them, as it is to learn a foreign language by simply reading a book on the subject and never trying to speak it. Nevertheless, if the instructions I have striven to convey in this little work are intelligently studied - and assiduously practised - by anyone ambitious to excel, they will assuredly assist him on the road to success and greatly lighten his journey.

By this time the pupil is becoming worthy of the name of a real student in the fascinating and Ancient Art of Juggling: and, if he can successfully manipulate three and four balls, he will need but little further instruction to enable him to juggle five or more. He must bear in mind the advice and teaching already given on the subject, as they apply to the successful playing of five or more balls just as much as they do to a smaller number. A few remarks, however, are called for regarding this more difficult work, as they may save much waste of time in useless practice.

---

22   A beautiful sentiment that is echoed in the work of many modern educators - without joy, much work is fruitless. It's pretty to think that Ingalese wrote this book in order to usher a new generation of jugglers into the world - allowing others to access the same "cheerfulness and pleasure" that he himself has enjoyed. (It's this attitude that led your humble editor to produce the book you hold in your hands, in fact! Is it vanity to think you have the same intentions as one of the forefathers of the craft? Perhaps. But here we are.)

The prettiest movements with five balls are those given at, the commencement of this chapter, viz. the Cascade, Shower, and Double- Shower.

To make good progress with five balls, the pupil should first perfect himself in the Cascade. This is practised much the same as with three, but with a much quicker motion.[23] Take three balls in the right hand and two in the left. Throw up a ball from the right hand slightly towards the left about a yard and half to six feet high, following immediately with one from the left: send another from the right hand and the next from the left, and while the first ball is just beginning its descent, send up the remaining ball from the right hand, and as each ball descends to the opposite hand return it again towards the other one. I think I hear my reader say "easier said than done." Quite right! Oh most wise Scholar! But if he apply himself steadily and systematically to the work but an hour or more each day, the results in a few weeks, providing he possesses any aptitude for the business, will be very encouraging. Make a point of counting, particularly when playing a number of balls, as it greatly assists in keeping good time, and you can also better note the progress you have made.

Showering five balls requires exactly the same motion as Showering four. Take three balls in the right hand and two in the left: play them as when playing four, except to throw them a little higher. It is best always to send up the first ball a little higher than the rest when Showering, as this gives more time to get the rest of the balls comfortably away. I would here emphasize the necessity of the Student keeping the best time in his practice that he is capable of. A simple and easy feat gone through in perfect time, with due regard to style and rhythm, may be more effective and pleasing than a much more difficult one played in a careless or slovenly manner without attention to time or style. It is an excellent plan to hum or whistle a favourite air to mark the rhythm in this practice.

---

23   See footnote 17 about heights, hand-speeds, and modern circus coaching. The same criticisms of Ingalese's approach also apply here.

Double-Showering is perhaps the most difficult of the three styles of Ball-juggling referred to at the beginning of this chapter.[24] The balls are thrown from the right hand to the left as in ordinary Showering, but those from the left hand to the right are thrown similarly, instead of being shot direct to the right hand. The balls thrown from left to right are kept inside those thrown from right to left in a smaller half circle. This is managed by the balls leaving the left hand not being thrown quite so high. It is a very showy feat and is accomplished as follows:- begin by Cascading five balls, and when you have got them running rhythmically, throw up one of the balls from the right hand over and outside the other balls to the left hand. When this can be successfully done, without interfering with the time, try two consecutive balls from the right hand in the same manner, viz. outside and over the others. This will of course require some practice but need not present any insuperable difficulty. Don't forget to send the balls from the left hand to the right a little lower than in ordinary Cascading. When the learner can throw two in this manner, he may try three, and so on, till he can throw all the balls leaving the right hand in an outer and therefore larger circle. This is the Double-Shower.

A very effective routine can be practised by the Student when he is versed in the three foregoing styles: by Cascading the five balls and counting up to, say twenty-five, then running into the Double- Shower and doing twenty-five, then finally into the ordinary Shower and doing fifty.[25] Of course the feats we are now describing require considerable practice, though that is no reason why they should not be mastered, but

---

24   This is another instance of changing juggling pedagogy. Most jugglers instructors in the 21st century would suggest five ball jugglers learn the cascade, then the "double shower" (half shower, in modern parlance) next.

25   Executing 50 throws of a five-ball shower is no mean feat - much more difficult than doing a simple 25 catches of a five-ball cascade... regardless of how modern jugglers count your shower tosses. (In siteswap, the five-ball shower is notated at *91*. Many jugglers only count the tall 9 throws, and not the 1s. In either case, it's a hard trick!)

my reader must not be discouraged if his progress is not so rapid as in the elementary stages. No man comes into the world a Juggler, and the feats of dexterity and skill that one occasionally sees and marvels at are the results of long practice.

To those of my readers who desire to excel in ball-manipulation, a few remarks on juggling six or seven may not come amiss.

Do not attempt Cascading six balls. The reader will call to mind what has already been said with reference to Cascading an even number of balls. Either practise a movement with three balls independently in each hand, as per instructions for four, or Shower with six. An artistic display is made with six balls by throwing up simultaneously two balls (one from each hand) about five or six feet high, so that they pass in the centre of ascent and descend to the opposite hands from which they are thrown. Immediately the first two leave the hands send up two more, and then the remaining two. Take especial care that both hands move exactly in unison, and that each two balls leave the hands simultaneously, and with the same amount of force imparted to them, so that they ascend to exactly the same height and travel at the same rate of speed. These points are essential to the effect of this graceful movement. In early practice it will often happen that the balls will collide, but this will soon be avoided with a little perseverance. I think this is perhaps, the most easily acquired and the prettiest of any six ball play in juggling.

To juggle seven balls, the Cascade is the best movement, and the only one which it is really possible to master. There are one or two well-known Jugglers who have attempted on the stage to Shower seven, but this is very exceptional.[26]

---

26   Juggling historian David Cain asserts that Frank LeDent was among these juggling greats who showered with seven. LeDent spent much of his career in Great Britain, so it's possible that if Ingalese ever saw the feat in person, it was LeDent! There were, however, other impressive ball jugglers working the

Double-Showering eight, or Cascading nine, is much easier than Showering seven; but playing eight and nine balls in these two respective styles necessitates years of practice, and I strongly advise my readers to apply their energies to making themselves expert with three, four and five balls, and with other articles and forms of the art, than to expend time attempting feats they probably will never be able to accomplish. It is, moreover, a painful fact in the experience of every artiste that it is not always the most difficult feat that finds most favour with an audience. I have often seen an exhibition of a marvellous performance, which has only been attained by years of laborious and painstaking application, scarcely evoke more than kindly applause, whilst some gaudy little trick learnt in the performer's apprenticeship days, showily done, has brought the house down. Juggling with any number of balls over five is a somewhat unreliable business. After years of practice, and when the necessary skill has been acquired, it necessitates unceasing practice to keep in form. I want my readers who take up these studies, to find in them a delightful recreation, and I would have them steer clear of attempting what they are very unlikely to succeed in mastering.[27]

European circuit at the time, including Chinko and Ameros Werner.
    27   Were your humble editor a cynic, he would insinuate that fair Ingalese was trying to dissuade young jugglers from getting better than him. But he isn't, so he won't.

Feats of Balancing

FEATS OF BALANCING FIND, I think, more favour with the embryo Juggler than any other branch of our beloved science. This is scarcely to be wondered at. To practise the Art of Balancing needs no spacious gymnasium, no mats, or balls. In the dingy office, or the spacious drawing-room, in bed-room or back-yard, articles galore await his attention. Pens and pen-racks, chimney ornaments and fire-irons, chairs and water-jugs, brooms and coal-scuttles, naught comes amiss to the budding equilibrist.

Whatever my reader's particular tastes may be, I sincerely and charitably pray he may not possess mine. For my special passion was for glass, china, or any similarly fragile article. The sight of such things tastefully displayed on a mantlepiece, or cunningly arranged in the recesses of a What-not, used to positively fascinate my sight. My nasal organ would itch to feel one or the other of them balanced on it, in apparent opposition to all the recognised laws of gravity and equilibrium.[28]

---

28   What a beautiful paragraph. This paragraph is an argument for the generative model of linguistics. Until this was written, no one had ever put these words in this order before. Your editor likes to think that Ingalese

When any particularly prized article was missing or discovered injured, I found the life of an aspiring Juggler not a particularly happy one. There is so little sympathy in this cold World with struggling genius, that it is perhaps as well not to encourage the desire to practise balancing chairs in a drawing-room! A slight trip may send the thing crashing through the chandelier or sweeping the mantlepiece. Better go, like a good and dutiful youth (which in sooth, beloved reader, I never was), to the back yard: where the thundering din of a coal-bucket falling off your forehead, nay even the entry of a broom through the kitchen window, will be sweetest music in your ears compared with the horrible jingle of mantle ornaments in the best room. Nor is the thought of the coming interview with Pater or Mater calculated to steady the nerves for further practice! I would, furthermore, affectionately remind the before-mentioned beloved reader that bulky vases and china ornaments are ill-adapted for the purpose - both by the laws of gravity and by those of economy. I almost weep at the recollection that my rudimentary knowledge, and (worse still) my later practice, was gained amid such surroundings and circumstances as I have referred to. My remembrance of some of the subsequent conferences on the subject of missing and damaged articles, is that they were of a nature peculiarly adapted to impress the memory. I trust these references to my early experience will deter the reader from following my evil example, and will remind him that there are more suitable places than nicely furnished apartments, and more serviceable articles than those of glass and china for the purpose.

But to get to business.

For the first lessons in Balancing nothing will be found better adapted than a common broom with a handle of from four to five feet long. For a novice this is an ideal article, the form and weight of the head greatly

---

approached his craft with the same artistry and attention to detail as these lines.

assisting in maintaining the equilibrium. The end of the handle should be rounded off, as it is far easier to balance than if left flat or jagged. Practice should be continued until the broom (or any similar article) can be balanced on the back of either hand with scarcely any apparent motion, and without the pupil having to move to and fro to keep it there.

Proficiency to this extent will be rapidly attained by the earnest Student, who can then practise balancing it upon his head. Commence with the chin, as there is less danger to the eyes from anything slipping than if the article were balanced on the nose or forehead. Of course the pupil will require a certain amount of practice before he can maintain an article poised on any part of his head or face; but he will quickly attain the necessary skill to keep any fairly long article (such as a broom handle) balanced for a few seconds on his forehead, nose or chin. When once he has acquired the knack of retaining it there but a couple of seconds or so, he will soon be able to keep it poised fairly steadily and without difficulty, for a long time, and without needing to move about.

Remember, it is chiefly at the start that learning anything fresh in juggling is discouraging.

In the particular branch of the Art we are now discussing, when the tyro has practised sufficiently to enable him to balance articles of different shape and weight moderately well his progress will be rapid. Needless to remind him again that opportunities for practice as well as articles to practise with, are practically unlimited. Anything, from a cigarette-paper to a dog-cart (presuming he possesses the necessary strength), may be utilised for the purpose. I may mention that much heavier and more unwieldy articles can be balanced on the chin than on the forehead or nose, and can be better controlled. Their being better seen than when on the nose or forehead assists greatly in enabling one to retain the equipoise. The chin, then, being particularly adapted for heavy-weight balancing should be gradually accustomed by careful and continuous practice with articles of increasing weight, to such burdens as the pupil cares, or finds himself able, to carry. Of course these remarks apply more particularly to those who purpose going in for heavy-weight balancing. The flesh of the face being very tender (and in some persons more than others) it would be easily injured or bruised if care were not taken and the weight carefully and gradually increased to the desired amount.

When balancing, keep the mind intently centred on the thing balanced and the sight fixed on the top of the article, Fig. 4. The Student who possesses the habit of observation will soon notice how much poorer progress he makes, when his mind is occupied with other matters, than when it is entirely centred on his work. This is true of all juggling practice but applies with especial force to balancing. To become an expert equilibrist the Student must cultivate will-power and the faculty of concentrating all the force of his mind on the work in hand.[29] The one

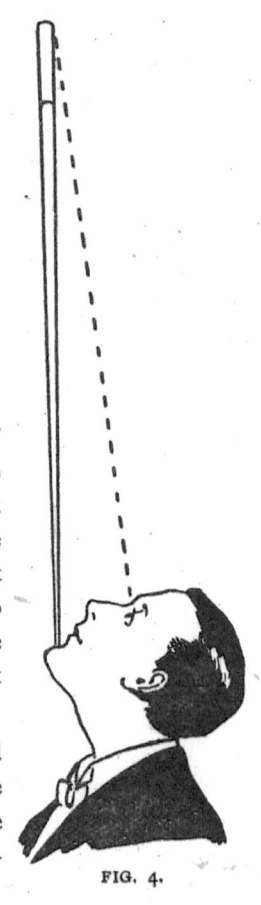

FIG. 4.

---

29   This remark reminds your humble editor of the following passage from an interview with the great Paul Cinquevalli, who died a few years before Ingalese's text was published:

> Perhaps the hardest thing a juggler must learn to do is to see things without looking at them. This may seem a paradoxical statement, but it is, nevertheless, true. For example, when I am balancing a glass on straw on my forehead, and juggling five hats at the same time I never look at the hats; if I did so for even the hundredth part of a second the glass and straws would collapse, but I know instinctively the position of the hats, and can catch them and juggle with them just as easily as if I were actually looking at them.

whose heart and pleasure is in his work will progress as much in one month as the listless worker will in three or even six months. But I suppose this applies to most things under the sun. To become successful in anything the brain must work as well as the muscles.

When balancing, have the head thrown well back so as to obtain the clearest view possible of the top of the thing balanced and to relieve all unnecessary strain upon the eyes.

The practice of juggling is very beneficial to the eyesight, as the various tender muscles of the eyes are kept in moderate and healthy exercise in the same way as are the muscles of the other parts of the body. The delicate and complex machinery of the organs of vision demand and deserve our especial care.

But it takes years of practice to acquire what I can only call this sort of double sight.

(Paul Cinquevalli, "How to Succeed as a Juggler," *Cassell's Magazine*, Vol. 47, No. 4, March 1909)

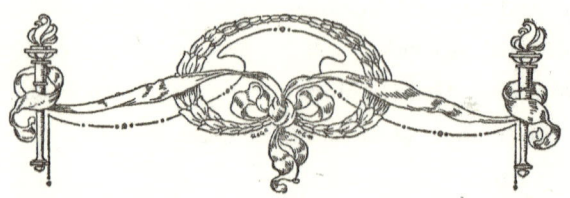

Juggling with Plates

JUGGLING WITH PLATES STANDS, perhaps, next in order of popularity. Unfortunately for the would-be Juggler's guardians, these articles are always to hand in the house, inviting to practice. But I would here advise my readers not to attempt proficiency in the use of plates by practising with the best china. Even common earthenware ones will be found expensive if they are to be constantly replaced. The hands, too, are liable to injury from breakage: to say nothing of the annoyance and trouble of clearing away the debris. The most suitable and satisfactory kind of plates are enamelled ones.[30] They are comparatively inexpensive, and with ordinary care will last a long time.

Do not get soup plates, but the common shallow dinner plates, from eight to ten inches in diameter. They can be obtained from any hardware dealer or ironmonger. When once accustomed to a certain form and weight of plate, it will be found advisable to adhere to the pattern very closely when purchasing fresh ones. It is a good plan to have a net, or

---

[30] American prop-maker Edward Van Wyck sold enamelled metal plates for this purpose in his catalogue at the turn of the 20th century. A set of three plates cost $1.50 (approximately $43.33 in 2019), and a set of one plate and one metal bottle cost $1.75 (approximately $50.55 in 2019). The latter set was specially-made for a series of tricks that will be mentioned later in this book.

something similar, stretched across where the plates fall when practising: as the constant dropping on a hard surface soon chips off the enamel, leaving the edges rough and jagged and unfitted for practice. Of course, the gymnasium mats before referred to, answer the purpose well.

In manipulating plates the same good old rule applies as to creeping before attempting to walk. A single plate is sufficient to begin with. It is to be held with the inside (or top) of the plate facing outwards, so that if held in the right hand the inside of the plate faces to the right: if held in the left hand, the inside faces to the left.[31]

It should be thrown straight upwards from the hand with a short quick throw, in such a way as to give it a spin or rotary motion towards the body. This will be naturally and rapidly acquired. Commence by throwing the plate about three feet into the air and catching it neatly again, between the fingers and thumb of the same hand. Gradually increase the height of the throw until you can throw a plate the height of ten or twelve feet or even more, and catch it again between the fingers and thumb of the same hand without moving from your position. You should be able to do this many times in succession. All heights of throw are to be tried, and it must not be forgotten to impart the spin so necessary to enable the plate to cleave the air without "wobbling," Practise first with one hand, and then with the other. When fairly proficient with each hand separately, practise with both it the same time: and continue to do this until you can perform equally well with both hands working at the same time as when working with either hand separately.

---

31   Yet again, we see Ingalese's penchant for putting showmanship over technique! However slightly convex, dinner plates fit most neatly in the hand with the inside of the plate resting against the thumb - showing the bottom of the plate to the audience. However, if you're juggling plates, Ingalese wants to make sure the audience sees plates - and the average person sees the top of a plate more often than the bottom, and therefore relates to it better in this orientation.

To learn to juggle two plates in one hand commence as follows. Hold one plate in the right hand and another in the left, the insides of both plates facing to the right. Throw up the plate in the right hand about six or eight feet high: and at once pass the other from the left to the right hand, and send it up after the first plate. Immediately the first plate is caught (by the right hand, of course) throw it up again, catch the descending one, send up the other and so on. As it is of importance that the first plate should be accurately dispatched, we start by holding a plate in each hand. It is not so easy if the hand is encumbered with the second plate: but, as soon as the tyro can keep two plates going for a few rounds, he may learn to start with the two plates in one hand as follows. The first plate must be held between the thumb and first finger, and the second plate between the first and the other fingers, both facing the same way - the upper outwards. Do not grip them too tightly. The second plate needs to be held a little more firmly than the first.

Send up the first plate, i.e., the one held between the thumb and first finger, not forgetting the spin: catch it and throw it up again, whilst still retaining the other plate between the first and second fingers. Practise until the plate can be thrown and caught with ease without losing a proper hold of the second plate. This will soon be accomplished and you can then proceed to practise properly, throwing each plate alternately and catching it again between fingers and thumb. In finishing a "round" slip the forefinger over the edge of the plate instead of throwing it up so that it is held between the first and second fingers - and make the last catch with the thumb and forefinger. Proceed in a similar way with the left hand until you can perform the feat equally well with it as with the right hand.

Having got thus far you will find juggling with four plates, two in each hand, come very easy with a little practice.

The two principal movements with four plates are neither of them very difficult. One consists in playing the plates simultaneously: that is, juggling two plates independently in each hand but throwing and catching them in unison. In the other movement one plays them alternately, leading off first with the right hand then with the left, then again with the right, and so on. The latter is perhaps the more effective. In both styles, the plates are played with the insides facing outwards: i.e., those in the right hand with the insides facing to the right, and those played with the left hand facing to the left, so that the fingers of each hand close on the insides of the plates, and the thumbs on the back.

When juggling three plates, using both hands and throwing them from one hand to the other, two are held in the right hand, and one in the left. The one in the left hand must be held so that (in this particular case) the usual order is reversed, and the fingers close on the back of the plate and the thumb on the inside. That is to say, when juggling from one hand to the other, the insides of all plates must face the same way, namely: to the right. Catching the plates in this manner with the left hand may be found a little awkward at first. Commence by throwing up the first plate from the right hand. Give each plate its proper spin and incline the throw towards the opposite (catching) hand. As plate No. 1 reaches the top of its flight, throw No. 2 from the left hand: and, as No. 2 reaches its height, catch No. 1 in the left and throw No. 3 from the right: and so on, over and over again, as long as you can. This movement is exactly the same as the Cascade with three balls. It is possible to work up a very pretty and easy routine in three-plate two-handed juggling.

To juggle three plates in one hand, hold them as just described for juggling three in both hands. Throw up the first from the right a little higher than the following ones, send up the second, take the third from the left hand and let it quickly follow the other two. They must be thrown a good deal higher than in juggling two. It will require considerable practice to master three in one hand as this is by no means easy: but the aspirant must remember "King Bruce and the Spider."[32] I must again emphasize the importance of giving the plates all the spin that can be imparted. In this movement, the plates have to ascend to a greater height, and it is necessary that they should be rid of all "wobble." The liability of the plates to collide, also, is a difficulty which will be experienced in this, as in other styles of juggling with plates; but the difficulty will soon disappear as the pupil acquires the knack.

The only practical method of juggling five plates is to play three in the right hand and two in the left hand separately.

The third plate is lightly held in the left hand by its extreme edge, between the tip of the thumb and the first plate. Commence by juggling two plates with the right hand only, until you have got them running smoothly. Then, throw both plates somewhat higher so as to give yourself time to take the loosely held plate from the left hand. As soon as the three plates are smoothly running in the right hand, commence juggling with the two in the left. If you have become proficient in the foregoing exercises and can play three plates with one hand, you will not require any further teaching or advice, if you are ambitious enough to try some of the higher flights of skill. You know now exactly how to begin, how to finish, and how to throw the plates. You lack nothing but the requisite practice, to perform the more difficult feats. You will naturally discover, too, in the course of the foregoing Exercises, many artistic little variations which you can add to your repertoire and use upon occasion to enhance your reputation.

The finest juggling with plates I ever had the pleasure of witnessing was during an engagement at Rotterdam. I arrived the day before I was to

---

32   "King Bruce and the Spider" is a Scottish folktale where the King of the Scots is inspired to go into battle *just one more time* in order to try for the nation's independence. He was inspired by a spider's perseverance in building his web, and ultimately succeeded.

open and I saw that another Juggler was advertised to appear in another Variety Theatre in the town. Having the evening off and being engaged to appear in a city, indeed in a country, I had never before visited, I was very curious to witness the kind of performance my brother Juggler would treat his audience to, particularly as it was his concluding night in Rotterdam. So I graced the rival Theatre with my presence. The artist's "turn" was throughout a very excellent one, but a good deal different from anything of my own until he came to plates. At this time I was making a specialty of plate manipulation, so I was greatly interested, and felt little doubt from what I had witnessed of his all-round clever juggling, that he would be skillful enough to play five plates. He did, and taking up another he held before his audience and my astonished self - six! Up to that night I had never witnessed an attempt to juggle with six plates. I had certainly heard of its being accomplished by a certain well-known artiste in the front rank of the profession Severus Schaeffer.[33] Six plates is a "tall order," but Mr Juggler gave a wonderful exhibition with his half-dozen. I was surprised and delighted, and at its close I expressed my thanks and pleasure by vociferously applauding. To my blank astonishment the man took up another plate and performed the phenomenal feat of juggling with seven. Seven! Again and again I found myself wondering if I was mistaken, but I was not. Now up to that time I had rather "fancied" myself in that particular line of juggling and it knocked considerable conceit out of me. Like Coleridge's Wedding Guest:

> "I felt like one who had been stunned
> "And was of sense forlorn,

---

33   Severus Schaeffer, Austrian-born juggling superstar from the turn of the century, was an extremely successful circus and music-hall performer. His acts included feats of strongman juggling as well as tricks and routines with household objects. One of his famous tricks, for example, was entering the stage in a small horse-drawn carriage. He would step down from the carriage, then lift it up and balance the whole thing on his chin. A full account of Schaeffer's act can be found in the December 1903 edition of Elias Stanyon's *Magic Magazine*.

> "A sadder and a wiser man
> "I rose the morrow morn."

I was still very young, so perhaps the kindly reader will regard my vanity lightly. I found there was a possibility of this "marvel" appearing the following night, so as soon as my turn was completed I hurried to the other Hall only to find he was gone, and was then en route for Germany. To one ignorant of, and uninterested in the Art, juggling seven plates may not seem an extraordinary feat: but it is really a marvellous piece of work. Juggling seven balls expertly requires an amount of skill that few artistes attain, but plates are much more difficult and the feat may be regarded as phenomenal.[34]

---

[34] It's a nice thought to believe this mystery juggler was Enrico Rastelli - the superstar Italian performer who performed eight plates in performance (according to the stories passed down from juggling phenom, Bobby May). However, juggling historian David Cain is quick to point out that Rastelli never performed with odd numbers of plates - only with six and eight (!). Frank LeDent, however, did perform with seven - as did Trixie LaRue.

Juggling with Bottles

JUGGLING WITH BOTTLES IS, to my mind, less effective than any other kind of juggling. From most points of view they are the least satisfactory of all the properties commonly utilised for juggling purposes. I shall not, therefore, deal at unnecessary length with the subject. To begin with, I strongly advise my readers not to use real bottles until they are fairly expert in the use of articles of similar shape made of wood or composition. Very awkward accidents may occur even to an experienced Juggler, owing to bottles colliding and breaking during manipulation. However, to those who desire to add tricks with bottles to their repertoire, I recommend champagne bottles. The glass is thicker than in the general make of bottles and their shape is better adapted for the work. Do not get the large size, but the size known as half bottles. The larger are altogether too heavy and cumbersome for ordinary work. In Juggling three bottles, they are held by the neck two in the right hand and one in the left The lead is naturally made with the right hand: the bottles are made to turn one revolution only and are caught again by the necks. There are many entertaining little tricks that will suggest themselves to the inventive tyro in bottle-juggling. An old and favourite one is Juggling three to the tune of "Weel may the Keel Row,"[35] or similar tune, while standing in front of a box, (a case made

---

35   This uptempo tune was a popular song in England and

to hold a dozen is a good size and very suitable for the purpose). After juggling the bottles a few times round whilst standing, gradually lower the body until the hands are not very far above the box, and complete the trick by keeping time to the music by striking the box with the bases of the bottles as they come into the hand.

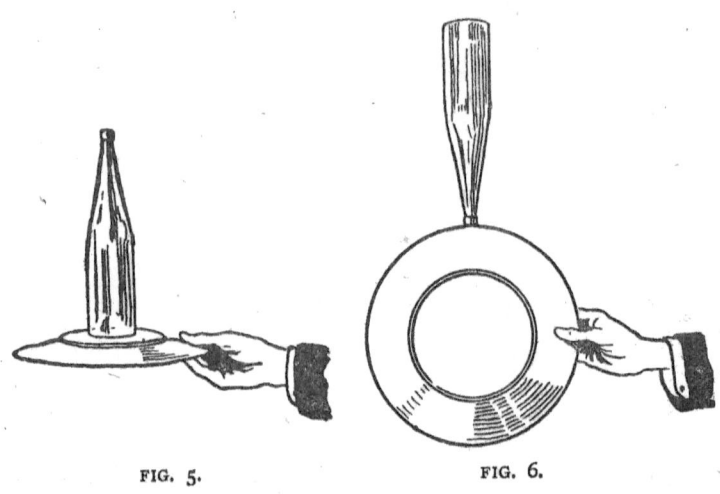

FIG. 5.   FIG. 6.

One of the prettiest effects in bottle-juggling, is produced by what is known as the Plate and Bottle Trick. This is done by holding an ordinary dinner-plate in the right hand, bottom upwards, with the bottle standing upon it, (fig. 5.) The bottle is then thrown half a turn into the air and when descending neck downwards is caught on the edge of the plate (fig. 6.) Though by no means one of the simplest movements it is not so difficult as it looks and is well worth the time it may require to perform it. A small hock bottle (half-size again) will be found the most suitable for the purpose: its peculiar shape tapering from base to neck being the better adapted to retain its equilibrium. These bottles can be obtained at any Wine and Spirit Stores for a copper or two. Having obtained one, the pupil must, with the point of a hammer or other tool fitted for the purpose, gently tap and chip the mouth of the bottle-neck so as

---

Scotland, and was often used to keep time in military marches.

to roughen its edge.[36] This, of course, will tend to prevent its slipping off the edge of the plate when caught there. First practise balancing the bottle on the edge of the plate. When the pupil can do this, the rest is easily learnt. Hold the plate with a firm grip with the fingers on the inside of the plate, and when throwing the bottle off do not throw it too high, just high enough for the bottle to take half a turn. When the bottle is thus thrown from the back of the plate and caught on the plate edge, balance it there for a few seconds and then throw it from the plate edge and catch it on the back of the plate again. This will be found somewhat easier than throwing it from the back of the plate and catching it on the edge. If the pupil is inclined to give the required time and attention to bottle and plate manipulation, he can vary his practice by throwing the bottle held by the neck from the left hand under his leg or round his back, and catching the neck of the bottle as before on the edge of the plate. In both these throws the bottle must be made to turn one complete revolution. Of course the final catch must be on the back of the plate, bottle upright as in the first position, and then with one of your "most sweetest" smiles at your audience and a little bow, replace the articles on your table and - "there you are." In this trick the pupil must guard against throwing the bottle too high. It only requires to turn one complete revolution, and should not be thrown higher than to take this turn "comfortably," as one might say. Until expert at bottle and plate tricks, the use of an enamelled plate will be advisable.

Another showy little exhibition is effected with two bottles, a plate and four liqueur glasses or small wine glasses. For this performance you require an assistant to pass the articles to you. Commence by balancing one of the bottles neck downwards on your chin or forehead. The plate,

---

36   Modern jugglers attempting this trick would do well to simply apply silicone tape or caulk to the lip of the bottle rather than attacking it (however gently) with a hammer. In contrast, Nikolai Bauman, author of the Soviet-era's textbook *The Art of Juggling*, simply suggests using a cork that extends "3-4mm over the glass rim of the bottleneck."

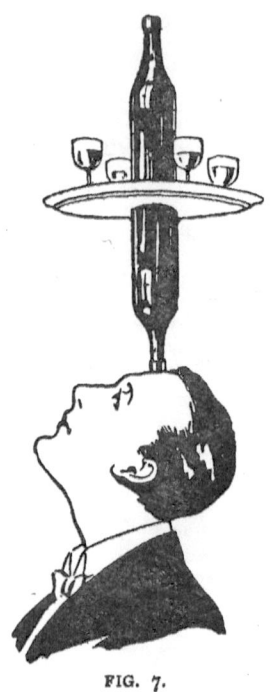

FIG. 7.

(as shallow a one as you can procure) and just sufficiently large to accommodate the other articles, is then passed to you, and placed by you, on the top of the bottle which is already balanced. Place the plate inside upward, just as it ordinarily rests on the table. Your assistant then passes you the other bottle which you place on the centre of the plate and then one by one the four glasses at equal distances on the plate round the bottle.[37] I remember regarding this trick in my young days as a wonderful instance of the equilibrist's skill, and it is always received with favour. It certainly is "gaudy"; but, if the pupil has become possessed of any knack in balancing it will be found infinitely easier to learn than it appears to be. One or two hints may be given that will be found worthy of notice. One is to fit a cork in the neck of the bottom bottle, cutting off nice and squarely any cork projecting above the neck. Also cut two circular pieces of linen slightly larger than the diameter of the bottoms of the bottles, and paste them on the top and bottom centres of the plates. These will be found not only to prevent to a great extent the tendency to slide, but will act as a guide in placing the plate and bottle centrally. Glasses with coloured tops add to the charm of this pretty drawing-room feat.[38]

---

37 Nikolay Bauman's 1961 book *The Art of Juggling* offers a variation of this trick that involves a bearing installed in the punt of the bottle. In this balance, the juggler can encourage the tray of glasses to slowly spin by taking the balance slightly out of alignment.

38 To your editor's knowledge, the only two jugglers currently presenting this feat on stage are British juggling icon Steve Rawlings and himself.

A Few Hints on Juggling with Clubs

MANY WELL KNOWN JUGGLERS specialize with Indian clubs; and this, in many cases, comprises their entire performance. When this is so, the act will probably include the full range of swinging,[39] sliding and ordinary juggling with 1, 2, 3 and 4 clubs: little additions being probably introduced by way of variety. There are of course many Club-Jugglers of the front rank who are clever in most of the other branches of the Juggler's Art, but it is rare to find one of exceptional ability equally good as an all-round performer. The reason is that this branch of work may be made to include such an infinite diversity of

---

39 The juggling clubs Ingalese is referring to here are not like modern juggling clubs. Indian club swinging was a popular form of exercise at the time of this book's writing and was even an Olympic event (last held at the Olympics in St. Louis, Missouri in 1904). These clubs were usually made out of solid wood and weighed several pounds each. These were not constructed with toss juggling in mind! That said, juggling historian David Cain is quick to remind readers that by this time, jugglers *were* using specially-made hollow wooden clubs, cork, and skeleton clubs. American prop-maker Edward Van Wyck made his clubs from white pine and had passed his club-making mantle to Harry Lind around this time, and it seems safe to assume that Lind used wood with similar properties. The clubs sold in the back of this book correspond to Van Wyck and early Lind weights, so they were likely hollow wooden clubs of a similar construction.

tricks and movements that its practice absorbs all the available time and attention that can be bestowed upon it. And it is worthy of it. I think there are few prettier "turns" presented on a Variety stage than a good Club act with tastefully decorated clubs.

To those of my readers who prefer going in for this form of juggling, a few remarks on the size and weight of clubs will be apropos. It will be found an excellent plan to use clubs of a certain size for particular classes of work. For instance, it will be found more convenient to use a certain size for one and two club work, and another for three. For those, however, who think of taking up clubs as a change and a variety in their ordinary juggling routine, one size and weight will be found sufficient. For one or two club work I recommend their being about 21 inches in length, 16 to 20 ounces in weight, and four-and-a-half to five inches in width. For working three clubs 19 to 20 inches in length, 18 to 19 ounces in weight and four to four-and-a-half inches in width; while still smaller are advisable for working four than for three. The form and weight of these articles are of the utmost importance for one taking up seriously the Art, and requires very mature deliberation. The aspirant will by this time have found the inconvenience attendant upon changing the size and form of articles used in practice after they have become familiar to his hand. This applies with equal or greater force to the branch we are now dealing with.

Having once become accustomed to a special shape and weight for certain work it must be adhered to, if at all possible, as hours of tedious practice are taken up in "breaking-in" a club of different dimensions. The weight of clubs varies considerably, and is largely a matter of personal preference. Some Jugglers prefer comparatively heavy ones while others fancy lighter ones. Of course a good deal depends on the age and strength of those they are intended for. A boy or girl of ten or twelve could not be expected to wield clubs suitable for a man. For very young people wicker-basket clubs are very appropriate. A few words on the manufacture of clubs may be acceptable.

Regarding their construction, there are several ways of making clubs or having them made. But the simplest method is to go to a good woodturner with the measurements and get them turned. Impress upon his mind that they must be turned out of the lightest possible timber. After the club has been turned in the solid, instruct him to drill or turn it out from the base. This is, of course, to lighten it as, even after this drilling out, the club will be found sufficiently weighty. But clubs made in this way can only be lightened to a certain extent. A half-inch wooden disc is fitted into the opening of the cavity and your club is ready for practice. Have only one made at first and, if perfect, it will serve as a pattern for any more you may require. If after using it a while you find it too heavy for three club use, it can be utilised for the work for which it is found best adapted (perhaps solo practice) and a set ordered with the measurements reduced. You must not allow Mr. Wood-turner to forget to use the lightest and softest wood, which, by the way, happens to be the cheapest: and, if as much as is practicable is turned out of the inside of the clubs, they should prove sufficiently light. If a jobbing woodturner is patronized where the work is done on the premises, it might be supervised and any suggestions offered during the progress of turning.[40]

Not much more need be said to aid the beginner in acquiring the Art of club-juggling. Much the same general advice and rules apply to this as to plate, ball and bottle manipulation. Obviously the first thing is to obtain a thorough familiarity with the size and weight of the clubs. Start with the solo practice for an hour or so daily, throwing it from one hand

---

40   There were dedicated juggling prop-makers at this time, but that equipment was expensive and sometimes required the referral of another working professional to be allowed to place an order. To learn more about the development of juggling clubs, refer to David Cain's *Juggling Props: A History (Vol. 1)*.

to the other, under and between the legs, over the shoulders and so on, taking care to use the left hand equally with the right. A good form of practice consists of throwing the club into the air first with one hand and then with the other, sometimes catching it with the hand that threw it, sometimes with the other. Endeavour always to catch it by the centre of the handle. At first throw it with only one turn between throw and catch, then try giving it two revolutions; first with one hand and then with the other, and sometimes catching it with the opposite hand. Take care, if the left hand is not the equal of the right in dexterity, to give it the larger share of the work: or even give it an hour or two's practice "on its own," if it is found to require it. When the club can be thrown with certainty three revolutions and properly caught, the pupil may regard himself as improving. These throwing exercises are very excellent practice for hand and eye. It is scarcely necessary to attempt more than three revolutions at present.

I would remind my readers of the wisdom of practising where the club may fall (when miscatching) on soft earth or mats, and so minimise the danger of its breaking. Since it is made of soft wood and is hollow, there is considerable risk of a club breaking if it receives a severe concussion from a high fall.

Our pupil may now take up two clubs to practise with, in all the ways his ingenuity can suggest. After a few days' exercise of an hour or two each day, our Juggler will have become on friendly terms with his clubs and he may now attempt three. As in all juggling tricks where an odd number of articles is brought into play the right hand should lead off. Two are taken in the right hand and one in the left. A good commencement is to throw one of the clubs held in the right hand, and catch it with the left (which, of course, already holds one) making it turn one revolution in its short journey and throwing it to the right again. It is as well to bestow a fair amount of time on this exercise before attempting to toss a second club.

I must again caution the reader against the tendency of throwing plates, balls, clubs, or other articles, too high.[41] As before pointed out, the movements of the article are slower and consequently less effective, and they are less under the control of the operator, and therefore played with less confidence and precision. Throwing clubs too high is most inadvisable. For one thing it calls for great judgment to make the throw with accuracy, and the time occupied in its flight gives it an appearance of slowness - the very opposite to that desired. It is easier to toss a club a yard high giving it one revolution than to throw it three yards high with one revolution. Don't forget to catch the clubs by the centre of the handles with a proper grasp, and do not catch it by the little knob on top with the finger tips.

With the foregoing hints and suggestions carefully noted and acted upon, it will depend upon the time allotted to practising, and the determination put into the work, as to what advancement is made within a stated time. Don't forget the advice given at an early stage in these studies, respecting the intimate relationship between concentration of mind on the work and assured success in any (or every) branch of work or play. I have before referred to the impossibility of learning juggling, or any other science, simply by reading a book. No man can become an expert pianist just by reading a pianoforte tutor, nor can you become an expert Juggler just by reading this book, without practice. One often hears it said, when a man has attained celebrity in any particular branch of Art or Science, that he is specially "gifted." I have generally found the "gift" to consist of love for the work and aptitude to settle down to steady, persevering practice and even hard labour, if necessary, to acquire the coveted skill. No sirs, no man is born a Juggler. It is an

---

41   Richard Kennison, juggling coach and recipient of the International Jugglers' Association's Excellence in Education award, is surely having a heart attack as he reads this line. As with most modern juggling pedagogues, Richard advocates that jugglers "embrace the height."

acquired Art - requiring similar qualities of mind and character to those necessary to enable a man to excel in any walk of life.

At an early age I had the good fortune to witness an exhibition by Charlene, a really marvellous Juggler, who manipulated a great number of balls: did astonishing tricks with hats, cigars, plates, and bottles: and concluded by dexterously juggling with lighted torches. This last was gone through with exceptional ability.[42] The fiery brands about him and around him mingled and intermingled with each other until nothing could be seen of the performer, who had gradually disappeared from view. A restless mass of fire circled in his place. To me it was a scene of enchantment most delightful to witness. I remember hearing it said that the man must have been specially gifted, or endowed by Providence, to attain to such a height of skill. Young as I was I had the intelligence to feel that such a theory, if acted up to, must have the effect of dwarfing my energies: and that I might as well throw up my beloved studies, unless I was satisfied to rest content as a fourth or fifth rate Juggler. This I was not content to be. I redoubled my efforts, discarding the theory of special gifts, and providential endowments: and found as others have found, that the only road to skill in Juggling, as in anything else worth striving for, is the royal road of perseverence.

"If at first you don't succeed - try, try, try again."

---

42   It seems likely that the Mr. Charlene referred to here is the male half of "Charlene & Charlene," referenced in an earlier footnote. In their November 3, 1903 review of his work, the *Sunderland Daily Echo and Shipping Gazette* offers the following words: "Charlene, billed as the 'master juggler,' certainly justified this claim. He gave his exhibitions in a [sic] easy fashion, which enhanced the smartness with which he performed different feats. The paraphernalia with which he juggled was varied, some of the articles being extremely awkward for the purpose."

Tricks with Hats, Umbrellas, Etc.

PROBABLY THE MOST FASCINATING tricks in all the range of juggling are those done with such articles as silk hats, umbrellas, walking sticks, cigars, etc. This branch of the Art equally enchants a drawing-room audience or one of costermongers, when gone through with fair skill, gracefully and with easy nonchalance. The number of tricks that can be performed with an ordinary tall-hat, a pair of gloves, a cigar and umbrella, is practically without limit;[43] and a special charm about this style of juggling is that often the simplest little feats are the most appreciated. Another advantage is that, once mastered, they do not demand such constant practice to keep in form as do most other kinds of juggling. Another point is that, should a slip or miss occur, it may be turned to the performer's advantage in such a way as to leave it doubtful whether the slip was really accidental or for effect - "as a blind," as the gallery would put it.[44]

---

    43   It's interesting to hear Ingalese's perspective here - Juggling with clubs is limited, but hats, canes, and cigars offer endless possibility. He would be surprised to learn that in 2019, only a handful of "gentleman" style jugglers remain and that circus artists are pushing the limits with clubs.

    44   "As a blind" is early 20th century slang for "as a ruse" or "as a deceit" - used here to say that the juggler had done it on purpose to make the routine look harder than it actually was.

Most Jugglers now commence their act with articles such as a hat and walking stick, cigar and gloves, etc., which are certainly appropriate to evening dress, in which a good many Jugglers now appear.

The well-known Max Cincinatti goes entirely through his splendid turn with nothing beyond these and similar impedimenta.[45] Some of the tricks performed by this and other artistes are wonderfully skillful, and have of course taken years to acquire, as in other advanced stages of the Art.

Before going further, let me refer a moment to the belief entertained by many people that all the articles used professionally by Jugglers are weighted at one end so that the weighted end comes down first. A minute's thought on this subject, at all events a minute or two's practice with weighted articles, will be sufficient to convince anyone of the folly of this idea; and to prove that it would require infinitely more practice to catch articles so weighted than when not weighted at all. There are a few things such as umbrellas, spinning bowls, billiard balls, and one or two others that can be "faked" to advantage, and this is dealt with in its due place; but in the great majority of cases the things employed are just as they are in ordinary use. However, to pass on to what is sometimes termed Modern Juggling, viz. - Silk Hat and Umbrella[46] work, etc.

---

45   Max Cincinnati was a comic juggler who worked from the late 1800s through the early 1900s. Your humble editor couldn't find much about Cincinnati, save for a handful of newspaper articles such as the January 19, 1899 edition of the *San Francisco Chronicle*, which called his juggling "one of the most attractive bits of the pleasant afternoon."

46   It should be noted that fake umbrellas were often employed by gentleman jugglers of this time. These were made out of turned wood, sometimes with a canvas covering. Fake umbrellas spin about the same as a stick or a club - they cannot be opened but look like the genuine article. Speaking as a juggler who has never actually handled Ingalese's props, I am fairly certain that he also used a fake umbrella. For reference, look at the photograph at the end of this book.

The first things required are, a tall hat, an umbrella or walking stick and a pair of gloves. The hat can always be obtained at a second-hand wardrobe-dealer's at a trifling cost. Get one to fit nicely, not too large, but just as if you were buying it for ordinary wear. Do not entertain the idea that a hat must be half-a-dozen sizes too large, so that it may the more easily "flop" onto your head when being caught. You might almost as well utilize a bucket for the purpose for all the artistic effect you would produce. Get as low a crowned one as possible; the higher it is the more difficult it is to catch or balance.

Next procure a pair of gloves of any thin material, cotton for preference. Roll them into a ball, and give them a stitch here and there to prevent them unrolling. The umbrella, or stick, follows next in importance. For general work a stick is preferable to an umbrella, and it is lighter and less awkward to handle. A very serviceable stick may be had from any wood-turner for a trifle. Have it the same length as your ordinary walking stick, of fairly light wood and slightly tapering. A medium-sized malacca cane makes an ideal juggling stick. Have no curved or crutched handle. An ornamental silver or gold mount is quite permissible, but this must not form any appreciable projection nor deviate from a straight line.

The kind of practice called for in taking up any new tricks will suggest itself to the pupil who has taken note of the advice and instructions already given. Practice means acquiring familiarity with any and all possible forms of juggling: and success means becoming proficient in each feat or "trick" before passing to one more difficult. Practise assiduously until a good balance can be maintained, as a good hat-balance will be found very useful in this class of work. Do not practise balancing it only inartistic, but useless from a practical point of view, to

FIG. 8.

FIG. 9.

balance hats on chins.[47] The correct place to balance a silk hat is on the bridge of the nose, (fig. 8.) Always keep your eye on the top edge of the brim. It is not so difficult to balance a hat as it appears when first attempted, and it will not take long to learn. In the figure, you will see that the crown of the hat, when balancing, is facing in the same direction as the performer. Rather more difficult is what is termed the "reverse balance," i.e., with the crown of the hat facing backwards (fig. 9.) In the "reverse balance" the hat must be placed at the junction of the nose and forehead so as to enable a sight to be obtained of the upper edge of the brim. The line of sight is indicated by the dotted line in fig. 9. The head must be thrown a little further back for this balance than for the preceding one, otherwise a view of the upper brim will not be obtained.

More difficult is the crown balance, which consists of balancing the hat with the edge of its crown resting on the upper part of the forehead (fig. 10.) This balance is by no means an easy on the chin. It is not one to retain, no view of its upper edge being obtainable. A good sight of the top

---

47   This advice runs parallel to that of Steven Ragatz of *Cirque du Soleil* fame. In his balancing workshops, he outlines the points of balance on the face - the chin is funny, as it moves when you talk. The nose is common and a great place to start. The forehead is dramatic, as your entire face is visible. We can assume that Ingalese does not like chin balancing with hats as it almost entirely obscures the face.

FIG. 10.

of the article balanced is not only a great aid, but practically indispensable. A very easy and effective little trick can be performed from this balance. Balance the hat as in fig. 9. Allow the hat to remain balanced for a second or two: then, letting it fall gently forward, it will be found that the brim will almost fall into the mouth. Catching the brim between the teeth, the hat can be tossed on to the head with a backward throw, making it turn one revolution.

Another neat comedy trick, which if smartly done never fails to "go," utilises the crown balance. First, take hold of the stick by the middle, with the right hand, and let the arm hang down by the side. Next, take hold of the hat with the left hand and place the edge of the crown on the forehead. Balance it there for a second and then allow it to fall backward: as it begins to fall, move the stick so that the ferule end points upward behind your back and catches the hat as it descends. This will be found quite easy after a little practice. It must be caught without any apparent effort, indeed as if it had dropped accidentally on to the stick.[48]

When a catch is missed, or by any mishap the hat falls to the ground, a neat way of making the best of the matter is to insert the toe inside the hat and throw it up with the foot. It is then caught on the stick or umbrella, whichever happens to be in your hand: or on the head for preference. Thus you can cover up a little mistake, and make it appear to your audience as if it were part of the "show." Of course, this throwing

---

48   If one would like to see this executed with expert finesse, one needs look no further than videos of Boris "Buba" Panfilenok, the expert Russian gentleman-style juggler who once received the Lenin prize for excellence in the circus arts.

up the hat "with a kick" will necessitate some preliminary practice, but it will be found quite easy. In case of the "glove-ball" dropping (gloves rolled into a ball for the purposes of juggling are called "glove-balls") walk calmly to it; and, gripping it with the inside of each heel, throw it forward over the right shoulder by a jump from the ground, and catch it in whichever hand you require it for the next trick. These methods of recovery will be found very easy and are very taking. They give an audience the impression that you are never at a loss with hand or foot to retrieve any little error you may make: even if they recognise that the article was not dropped on purpose! It also imparts a touch of humour that is always admired in a "straight" juggling act.

A straight Juggler is one who relies entirely upon his ability in performing genuine feats of skill to interest his audience. The Comedy Juggler on the other hand, does not always possess sufficient talent, and so affects a funny makeup (often of the genus tramp) and endeavours to amuse his audience by performing in a droll manner. Of course, there are notable exceptions to this rule. For example, that well known Juggler, W. C. Fields,[49] who gives a most wonderful performance in such a quaint and humorous manner that it appeals irresistibly to the risible faculties of his audience, while at the same time leaving them marvelling at his extraordinary dexterity.

---

49   W.C. Fields, born William Claude Dunkenfield, was a famous juggler-cum-actor in the early 1900s. He first entered the Vaudeville stage in 1898 and continued performing on stage, radio, and film until his death in 1946. For more on Field's extraordinary life and career, refer to James Curtis' biography *W.C. Fields: A Biography*.

The Hat and Cigar Trick.[50]

FIG. 11.

Very few Jugglers, especially those who perform in evening dress, omit to make use of the cigar. Of course, there are many tricks that can be performed with the cigar alone, but undoubtedly the best is in combination with the hat. There are few Jugglers who at one time or another have not made a feature of this trick: and although certainly not new, it is always received with favour. It is accomplished by placing a silk hat on the end of an umbrella, or stick, and a cigar on the hat, as in fig. 11. The hat and cigar are thrown off the stick simultaneously and the hat is, of course, caught on the head and the cigar in the mouth, (fig. 11.) The umbrella, or stick, should be held about its middle; and the hat and cigar thrown off the end with an easy upward movement. This should be done exactly the same as if the hat were going to be thrown

---

50   If you'd like to see modern masters of hat and cigar work, look no further than Olivier Caignart, Dan Gorski, Kristian Kristoff, and Kris Kremo (listed in no particular order).

on to the head without the cigar. It is essential that the cigar be placed correctly, the thick end resting against the brim of the hat. It is best to practise catching the cigar in the mouth first, as this is the most difficult part of the trick. The cigar must be caught first, as it has not so far to travel: but the hat is caught immediately after. Place hat on end of stick, or umbrella, and cigar on hat, and throw both articles in the manner explained. As the cigar parts company with the hat, try and catch the end of the cigar in the mouth, not attempting to catch the hat to begin with. When the cigar can be fairly often caught, then practise catching the hat at the same time. It is advisable for beginners, as pointed out, to catch the hat on the back of the head. It is easier, and gives the performer a fraction of a second longer between catching the cigar and catching the hat.[51] A deal depends on the length of the cigar. I recommend a length of five inches. This can be easily fashioned out of a piece of wood[52] and will be found very serviceable for practice. For "show" purposes (that is, when before an audience) have one turned out by a wood-turner. A showy cigar-band round adds greatly to the deception. Any wood-turner will make such a cigar for a few coppers. There is little occasion to paint it. A few hours' practice will take off the newness, and leave it pretty much the colour of an ordinary cigar. Have it made out of soft wood.

There are just a few tricks that Jugglers perform in which it is advisable to "fake" slightly the articles used: although it is not always necessary, and "faking," or preparing, does not always render the article easier to use. Take, for instance, the Hat and Cigar trick. Very

---

51   Although Nikolay Bauman's *The Art of Juggling* does mention this trick, the book simply instructs his readers to "throw the cigar and hat off the cane with a single flip. Then catch the cigar with your teeth first, and the hat with your head afterward."

52   Nota bene - If you're interested in working on this trick, do not make a cigar out of bamboo. Bamboo - while an easy and light wood to work with - flexes a great deal. The technique used in this style of "mouthstick" work requires a fair amount of tension in the front teeth - bamboo can flex and rebound between your teeth and crank your teeth right out of your head.

few Jugglers perform the feat with, a real cigar. Most of them, as I do myself, use a "property" cigar; not because it renders the trick easier of accomplishment, but because it is always to hand, and ready for use. It is just as easy to perform with a real cigar.[53] On the other hand, there are some tricks where a little clever "faking" makes the trick much easier.

The Eyeglass Trick.

A very entertaining and pleasing little feat, and one always sure of appreciation, is done by throwing up a coin from the foot, catching it in the eye and retaining it there as an eyeglass. I recommend this trick, as it requires but little practice and no great space in which to perform it. The chief thing required is a coin to fit the eye. When performing this trick, I use a half-crown piece; but for many of my readers this coin will be too large. A penny filed down to the requisite size makes a good substitute.[54] A fairly new coin should be utilized, as the heavier the coin the easier the trick. The edge must be "milled" all round with a file, as this enables the muscles of the eye to get a better grip than if the edges were left smooth. The coin can be silvered, or nickel-plated, to give it a more artistic appearance than copper. The coin should be placed on the centre of the toe of the right boot. The foot is then slightly lifted off the floor and held a little forward while the body is balanced on the left foot. After a momentary pause in which to judge the distance, throw up the coin above the forehead. It is unnecessary to throw the coin more than six inches or so higher than the head. As it is just on the point of

---

53   Many juggling prop manufacturers at the turn of the century offered prop cigars for this kind of work. Some companies also offered cigars made from solid metal to be used in a one-off gag where the cigar was dropped on the floor and the sound echoed around the theater!

54   Coinage has changed substantially since this book was written. The half-crown Ingalese talks about measured 32mm in diameter. The penny measured 31mm across. For reference, the American half dollar measures slightly over 30mm in diameter.

descending on the forehead drop the body a little at the same instant, to prevent the coin bouncing off. The head must be thrown well back as the coin is caught on the forehead-just above the nose, when possible. When the coin is resting in this position gently shake it down over the right eye (or the left, if the reader has more control over its muscles). When the coin is over the eye, open the eye fairly wide; and then close down the muscles over the edge of the coin, still with the head well back. A little preliminary practice at holding the coin, or a monocle, in the eye in the ordinary way is desirable. A neat way of introducing this trick is to take the coin from the waistcoat-pocket. After the coin has been thrown off the boot, caught in the eye and retained there long enough to obtain the due effect, it can be dropped into the waistcoat pocket again by just holding the pocket slightly open with the first finger and thumb and releasing the coin from the eye.

FIG. 12.

A trick invariably well received is executed with hat and umbrella. In this, the brim of the hat is balanced on the nose, and while in that position the umbrella, or stick, is laid across the hat resting on its brim and the edge of its crown. (Fig. 12.) An ordinary umbrella will give but little difficulty, as it has very little tendency to roll off; but the stick will

be found a more difficult matter. The amateur will find it possessed by a "demon of unrest" prompting it to roll off. The difficulty can however be got rid of by the aid of our friend the wood-turner. Get him to cut a groove along the stick-not necessarily its full length. This will aid both in placing the stick in position and keeping it balanced there: the two edges of the groove resting on the brim and the edge of the crown, as in Fig. 11. The groove will not be visible to the audience.

This makes a charming opening trick: for, while the hat is balanced with the umbrella on top, the hands are at liberty to remove gloves, overcoat, etc. Then calmly, with a slight forward movement of the head, let the hat drop into proper position. The umbrella will slide down behind, when it can be caught without any apparent effort as it falls towards the floor, by the right hand being slipped round to the back.

I would strongly advise those of my readers who intend specialising in this particular branch of the art (often known as "Modern Juggling") to practise Three Hat Manipulation. It is a very good addition to one's repertoire, anyway; and is always certain of appreciation. It is absolutely essential, first, to be able to throw a hat from either hand and catch it neatly on the head. Hold the hat with the fingers partly inside, crown upwards, and the thumb on the top side of the brim. Throw it so that it turns one complete revolution, and drops comfortably into position on the head. As the hat is caught, the body should be slightly dropped (by bending the knees at the same second of time) so as to break the force of its impact and prevent the hat bouncing off should the throw be slightly faulty. If this cannot be accomplished with ease it must be practised until it can.

For the three hat work three silk hats are all the is props required. Some prefer opera-hats. They should be as nearly as possible the same size, shape and weight: and should be about half a size larger than the

FIG. 13.

performer's usual size, so as to sit fairly loosely on the head.[55] Amongst the many different styles of hat manipulation, one of the easiest and yet most artistic is the following.

Place one hat on the head, slightly at the back: and hold one in each hand, as in Fig. 13. Bend the body slightly forward. Throw the hat from the right hand so that it can be caught on the head; but before it reaches the head, the one already there must be snatched off by the same hand. This must be done very rapidly, as there is very little time between the hat being thrown and its being caught. Snatching off quickly and correctly is of the greatest importance, The real difficulty lies in the fact that the hand which throws hat No. 1 is also the hand which snatches off No. 2. But this difficulty, like others, must be overcome by practice. The best way to remove the hat quickly is to take hold of the front part of the brim with the fingers underneath and the thumb on the top. The knack of twisting the arm so as to get the correct hold necessitates some little practice, but it will soon come. The advantage of this method is that, even as the hat is removed, it is already in the correct position for being thrown again. As soon as hat No. 1 is thrown from the right hand, No. 2 removed, and No. 1 caught on the head: No. 3 from the left hand must be thrown and No. 1 snatched off to make room for it. When No. 3 is caught, the one from the right hand must be thrown again and so on. Keep the head well back, with the shoulders forward.[56]

It is advisable to catch the hats somewhat on the back of the head, as this makes it easier to snatch them off: and it also leaves the sight unobstructed by the brim. The instructions given about dropping the

---

55   Anecdotally, juggling superstar Kris Kremo goes through dozens of silk hats every year. These are simply off-the-shelf top hats which have the brims reinforced with a stiff plastic interface. Your editor wishes he had a similar budget for haberdashery.

56   If you'd like to see this trick performed well, look no further than videos of   Kris Kremo, Kristian Kristoff, Wally Eastwood, Dieter Tasso, and Shirley Dean.

body each time a hat is caught on the head must not be forgotten. If you are being accompanied by music, don't attempt to keep time with the instrument, but instruct the musician to keep time with you.

There are many other movements in juggling with hats, and should any of my readers purpose making a specialty of this particular line they will find little difficulty in originating tricks and movements innumerable with three hats. At any rate, once you know how it is done, you will be able to copy any new "trick" you may see done by a professional Juggler.[57]

The Matchbox Trick.

Another showy little feat is the taking of a match out of a matchbox, throwing up the box a foot or so into the air, and lighting the match by striking it on the box as it descends. This scarcely requires practice. The secret is in the way the matchbox is prepared, or "faked." Get a few boxes of safety matches (Swedish for preference[58]) and take off from two or three of them the sides used for striking the matches on. Glue these on to one of the match-boxes so as to cover the entire box. A match can now be struck on any part of it. All that is necessary is to take out a match, throw up the box: and, as it descends, simply take care that it hits the business end of the match you hold, which will immediately ignite. Remember in the preparation of the trick: (1) Choose a matchbox that fits together firmly. You do not want it to slide open and scatter matches in all directions during your performance. (2) Glue on the prepared sides with good strong glue, and let it get hard and dry before

---

57   Well, knowing *how it is done*, plus considerable effort and years of practice!

58   At the turn of the century, matches produced by Jönköpings och Vulcans Tändsticksfabriks Aktiebolag were considered some of the safest and most reliable matches in the world. For your purposes, any "strike anywhere" match should do!

putting the matches in. (3) See that the box is filled with fresh matches, which have had no chance to get damp. Having the box full, of course, makes it heavier and so it will strike your match for you more easily in its descent. Remember in the performance of the trick (1) Look carefully at the match you take out of the box. This will give the audience time to see that you really have a match in your hand, and will give you time to see that its head is sound. A "dud" would spoil your trick. (2) Hold the match firmly, and close to the "business" end, to avoid any danger of its breaking on coming into contact with the box.

Another way of springing a little surprise on an audience is by putting the hand into the pocket and taking out a lighted match. This is very simple. All that is required being a piece of rough sandpaper, two or three inches long by half as wide, sewn inside the outside pocket of the coat. Put a few ordinary (not safety) matches into the pocket, and all you have to do is to put your hand in your pocket, and take hold of a match: strike it on the sandpaper as you withdraw your hand, and the thing is done. Have the sandpaper sewn on the inner side of the pocket, so that when the match is struck it can be pressed against the body. The above are, of course, Conjuring tricks rather than proper Juggling: but graceful and novel styles of lighting a cigar or cigarette during a performance always interest an audience. Such little "tricks" both serve to fill intervals between two pieces of "business" and give variety and lightness to your "show."

Never keep your audience waiting: your "turn" will be judged and appreciated for its smooth working from beginning to end, as much as it will for the cleverness of its tricks. One of the great failings of amateurs on the stage, or platform, is their bad habit of keeping an audience waiting both before beginning their "turn" and whilst changing from one trick to another.

Never keep your audience waiting. Be "on time" with everything.

Addendum

IT HAS OCCURRED TO me in the writing of the foregoing pages, that perhaps many of my readers will experience a certain amount of difficulty in obtaining the necessary properties, or "props" (for short) as the goods suitable for Juggling practice and performances are called. We find in the profession that the home-made article seldom gives real satisfaction; and goods bought at shops, where they profess to understand the manufacture and use of such articles, are of little (if any) more utility. Juggling "goods" to give perfect satisfaction should be made by one who thoroughly understands their use, and who is acquainted with the particular tricks for which they are intended.[59] Very many hours of practice may be saved, if properly made "props" are used. I remember what it cost me in my early days, both in pocket and in time wasted at practice, through not knowing where to get such articles as every would-be juggler must possess. I was continually visiting wood-turners, tinsmiths, etc., and buying "props" from people who obviously didn't know the difference between a Conjuror and a Juggler. It was not until I became personally acquainted with a "real live professional juggler" that my troubles were to some extent at an end. This juggling friend of mine "put me wise," as our American cousins would say, to innumerable little wrinkles as to how to make, and get made, certain articles that I had never dreamt of. I certainly should never have found out in the ordinary course of events, and I might have gone on practising in the old way for

---

    59   This is extremely important for any juggler to know - whether they live in the 20th century or the 21st. Your humble editor suggests that all jugglers - no matter the discipline or artistic inclination - learn how to build and maintain their own props. You never know when something will be lost or damaged on the way to a show, and you'll thank yourself for having such an intimate connection with the tools of your trade.

a lifetime; for such performers as my friend are rarely met with. It is very seldom one is encountered who will give away the "little secrets" of his business. Although there is much less "faking" than many people think in the manufacture of Juggling "props," there is a great deal in how the "props" are made to lessen the risk of failure.[60] This even applies to such ordinary things as the plates and balls used in the most familiar of all juggling tricks.

Many will think, no doubt, that it is just as easy to juggle with wooden and rubber balls of different sizes or weights, as it is with any other kind: but let me quickly correct my reader on this point. Hours and hours of practice may be saved by commencing to learn ball-juggling with the right size and weight of ball. The same applies to plates and to every other article that it is possible or likely that the budding Juggler will use. It is with the idea of helping those of my readers who really intend taking up juggling either as a hobby or with a more serious view in mind, that I have decided to save them the trouble and worry that I had to go through (the same no doubt that many of our best known Jugglers also experienced) by suggesting to the publishers of this little work to arrange the manufacture of a few of the most needed "props" the amateur is likely to require. This, I am pleased to say, they have agreed to do and I assure my readers that all articles and tricks mentioned in the following small catalogue are made by experts in the manufacture of juggling "props" and are guaranteed to be exactly the same in every detail as those used by many of our finest Jugglers.

I may add that in my present act I use a number of these articles, namely, the juggling candle and candlestick, a spinning basin, the imitation umbrella, a cigar and a set of torches, etc., all of which give me complete satisfaction.

---

60   Once again, Ingalese offers wisdom. It's not about a "trick" that makes a particular juggling feat work - it's about finding the props that are most favorable to success.

JUGGLING GOODS.

As supplied to the Leading Jugglers in the profession.

All goods are specially made of the finest materials by experts, and all articles are thoroughly tested before being sold.

> **Terms**—Cash with order. Always send Postal Orders or Post Office Money Orders crossed & Co., and made payable to—
>
> "GOODS DEPT., GASGARTH PRESS."
>
> N.B.—Postal Orders and Treasury Notes should be sent per *Registered Post* to ensure safe delivery.

All goods are sent *carriage paid* in the *United Kingdom*. Carriage extra on all overseas orders.

Juggling Goods—*Continued.*

Ball and Two Sticks,
12/6
Easy and effective to use.

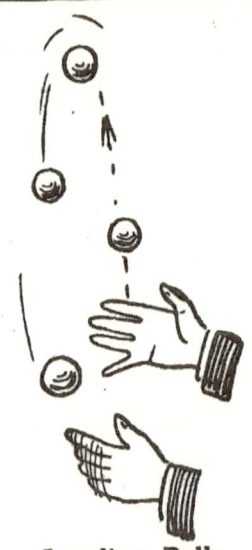

Great Comedy Cannon Ball Trick.
2 solid and 1 rubber.
Black finish. Always a big laugh in any act.
The Set 16/-

Brass & Nickle-plated Juggling Balls to order.
Prices on application.

Juggling Balls.
Made of boxwood, correct size and weight. Finished like billiard balls. Set of three, two white and one red
12/6
Extra balls **4/6** each.
State colour required.

Best Rubber Balls for Ball Bouncing
Each **4/-**   Set of three **11/-**

Metal Juggling Basins.
Specially made for spinning on a stick or for ordinary Juggling. Nicely decorated. Professional size.
17/-
Stick for same **3/6**

Candlestick & Juggling Candle.
Accurately made to make trick very easy, with special "fake" for using candle lighted if required. Very highly finished.
14/6
Separate Candles **3/6** each.

Juggling Goods—*Continued.*

Packing and Carriage Free on all orders in the United Kingdom. Carriage extra on Foreign Orders.

Juggling Torches.
New fire end, always ready for use. Merely require oiling. The finest on the market.
Set of Three, 45/-
Correct length and weight.

EXTINGUISHING Box for Torches, made in strong sheet tin. Indispensable for those using torches. Bound with brass. Enamelled in red.
25/-

Rolling Ball on Stick.
Apparently a fine feat of balancing, but really quite simple. Requires but little practice.
7/6

Juggling Cigar.
Made in soft wood so as not to hurt the teeth. Can be smoked like a real cigar and is finished to look exactly like one. "Faked" for resting on brim of hat.
5/- each.

Plate and Bottle Trick
Specially made wooden bottle, finished to look like the real thing. Correctly weighted. Splendid for preliminary practice. The bottle and metal plate
10/6

Juggling Goods—*Continued.*

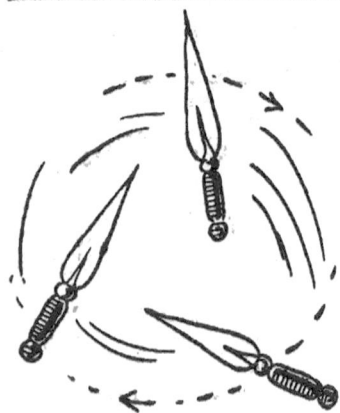

Juggling Clubs.

The finest in the world. These clubs are covered with fine quality canvas, have hardwood handles and are practically unbreakable. They are beautifully decorated, ready for professional use, and are very light, the weight being only about 16 ounces. They are 21 inches long, and are identical with those used by all the leading Club Jugglers.

Set of Three, 55/-

Single Clubs, 20/-

Juggling Knives.

The finest obtainable. Very accurately made and balanced. Nickle-plated blades. Very handsome in appearance.

Set of Three, 55/-

Imitation Juggling Umbrella.

Looks exactly like the real thing. Grooved for balancing on hat. Handle is ivory finished. A very useful addition to a Jugglers' stock-in-trade. Made in good hard wood.

Each 10/6

Trick Billiard Balls and Cue.

Appears to be a wonderful feat of balancing skill, but in reality it is quite simple and requires very little practice.

Price complete with two balls and cue and full instructions

21/-

Juggling Goods—*Continued.*

> *SPECIAL ATTENTION is called to the fact that all goods advertised in this catalogue are made by experts who thoroughly understand the manufacture of Jugglers' Requisites and all are perfectly made and finished in "true professional style" ready for stage or private use.*

Basket Juggling Clubs.
Very useful for ladies and for juggling more than three. Also for double club juggling, passing, preliminary practice, etc.
Covered with strong linen. Extra light.

Set of three, 30/-
Single Clubs, 11/-

Metal Eyeglasses.
Nickle-plated and milled edge for catching in the eye.
Correct size. Each 2/-

Juggling Plates. Metal.
Decorated, useful size.
Set of three 8/6
Single Plates 3/- each

Boards for Bouncing Balls, 2 ft. 6 in. long, 1 ft. 4 in. wide. Hinged in centre for folding. Black Bordered. **21/-**

| All goods sent carriage paid in the United Kingdom. | Heavy Nickle-Plated Cannon Balls specially made to order. Prices on application. | Carriage extra on all orders from Overseas. |

TERMS.—Cash with order. Send Postal Orders or Post Office Money Orders (crossed & Co.,) made payable to:—Goods Dept., Gaskarth Press.

N.B.—Postal Orders and Treasury Notes should be sent per Registered Post to ensure safe delivery.

ADDRESS—

GOODS DEPARTMENT,
GASKARTH PRESS
Balham, London, S.W. 12
ENGLAND.

You would like to take Notes in Shorthand—but

(1) it takes so long to learn Shorthand, and
(2) you can't be sure of reading it when you've written it.

WHY NOT TRY SONOSCRIPT?

THE NEW SPEED-WRITING.

Simpler than Shorthand.   Legible as Longhand.

60 words a minute in three months.

"All About It" and Free Lesson (postage 2d.)

Write, Scribe J.G.

The Sonoscript Society,
55 & 56, Chancery Lane,
W.C. 2.

Correspondence Course £2 10s 6d post free, or 10/6 weekly.
The Little-Lesson Book 2/8 post free.

Classes—New Term begins January, 2, 1922.

Write for Particulars.

CAN YOU SPEAK IN PUBLIC?

"The Science and Art of Speech."

Five Lectures by Dr. F. L. SESSIONS.

Verbatim Reports now ready, 2/6 each Lecture.

Write for Syllabus to Scribe J.G.,
The Sonoscript Society,
55 & 56, Chancery Lane, W.C. 2.

White Bros.

SUCCESS
THE NAME TO JUGGLE WITH.
IF
YOU WOULD BE A SUCCESSFUL PERFORMER
YOU
MUST HAVE GOOD PROPERTIES, AND TO TRAVEL GOOD PROPERTIES YOU **MUST HAVE** A GOOD HAMPER

Wires—"HAMPERS," Nottingham.   Phone 744.

The Strongest, Safest and Most Durable Hampers in the World
Are made by the Firm with the Successful Name—

White Bros.

THE HAMPER MAKERS,   **81 PARLIAMENT STREET, NOTTINGHAM.**

Send for Catalogue.

YOU CAN PLAY THE PIANO TO-DAY

BY

Naunton's National Music System....

IT makes no difference whether you have had previous lessons or not, whether you are 80 years of age or only 8, we guarantee that you can play the piano to-day by this wonderful and simple system. There are no sharps, flats, or theoretical difficulties to worry you, and no tiresome or wearisome exercises or scales to be learnt. You play correctly with both hands at once. No difficulty or drudgery whatever.

FAILURE IS IMPOSSIBLE.

'You cannot fail." All you have to do is to sit down to the piano with our music and play it at once—Hymns, Dance Music, Songs, Classics, anything.

Over 50,000 people are playing by it, and are playing perfectly. If they can do it so can you.

If you are one of the thousands who have tried and failed, have given up learning by the old methods owing to the difficulties, or if you are afraid to begin because of the drudgery, let us tell you all about this wonderful, simple, rapid and perfect system, which is a real educator. The word "educator" means "to lead out" or "to draw out." It does not mean "to cram in." Our system draws out the musical powers of our students from the very first lesson. Take advantage of the offer we make on the coupon below, and by return of post you will receive eight tunes, which we guarantee you can play; thus you can prove for yourself the simplicity of our system and the accuracy of our statements. This small outlay will open up the delights of the vast realm of music to you and give you many years of purest pleasure.

No one need ever say again, "I wish I could play"; everyone can do it, to-day.

Cut along this line.

SPECIAL TRIAL OFFER COUPON.

To the Manager, Naunton's National Music System, *Juggling,*
7 Newman St., Oxford St., W.1. *1921.*

Being a reader of JUGGLING and desiring to test your system, I send herewith postal order for ONE SHILLING AND SIXPENCE, in return for which please send me your "Special No. 1," published at 2s 6d, containing eight tunes, with instructions how I can play them at the first sitting, also your special Booklet and particulars of how I can become a thorough musician.

NOTE.—Please fill in postal order payable to *Naunton's National Music System Ltd.*
Colonial readers, British Postal Orders only accepted.

Name ....

Address ....

Date ....

The Gaskarth Press

(GOODS DEPARTMENT)

TERMS—Cash with Order.

Always send Postal Orders or Post Office Money Orders crossed & Co., and made payable to

"**GOODS DEPARTMENT,
GASKARTH PRESS.**"

To ensure safe delivery all letters containing money should be sent per Registered Post.

All goods sent carriage paid in the United Kingdom

The Gaskarth Press

(GOODS DEPARTMENT)

Balham, LONDON, S.W. 12
ENGLAND.

Juggling Props, comprising Gintaro's Amazing Spinning Top, a wooden candle and candlestick, and an umbrella, both originally the property of Rupert Ingalese (also known as Paul Wingrave); and a ball and pedestals that belonged to Herbert J. Collings "Col Ling Soo." Photograph courtesy of David Cain.

Acknowledgements

This little book wouldn't have been possible without the help of the following people (listed here in alphabetical order.)

Becky Brown
David Cain
Benjamin Domask
Kate Peterson Koch
Will Menarndt
Nathan Wakefield

OTHER TITLES BY MODERN VAUDEVILLE PRESS

Juggling - From Antiquity to the Middle Ages
by Thom Wall
ISBN: 978-0578410845

As with dance, so with juggling—the moment that the performer finishes the routine, their act ceases to exist beyond the memory of the audience. There is no permanent record of what transpired, so studying the ancient roots of juggling is fraught with difficulty. Using the records that do exist, juggling appears to have emerged around the world in cultures independent of one another in the ancient past.

Paintings in Egypt from 2000 BCE show jugglers engaged in performance. Stories from the island nation of Tonga place juggling's creation with their goddess of the underworld—a figure who has guarded a cave since time immemorial. Juggling games and rituals are pervasive in isolated Inuit cultures in northern Canada and Greenland.

Winner of Next Generation Indie Book Awards - "Best Nonfiction eBook" 2019

A friend once asked me, 'What's the point of juggling three or five balls?' None, really, besides that not everybody can do it. Yet, juggling is one of humanity's oldest performing arts; it seems that every civilization known to man has produced amazing people who have successfully tried to keep objects moving simultaneously in the air in defiance of all laws of gravity. So, where does juggling comes from? When did it begin? What is its history? These are the questions Thom Wall has endeavored to answer in his fascinating book, Juggling From Antiquity To The Middle Ages. Thoroughly researched, richly illustrated, Thom Wall's book is a must-read for anyone interested in juggling or the circus arts in general, anyone interested in performing arts, and anyone with a curious mind.

- Dominique Jando, author, The Circus (1870-1950)

Body Talk: Basic Mime
by Mario Diamond
ISBN: 978-1-7339712-1-8

From the foreword: The art of mime is the identification with the essence of all things, and the portrayal of thought and emotion through silent physical expression. A mime works with the laws of physics: weight, gravity, principles of motion and resistance and inertia. We move through space as a visible, tangible substance.

Mime training is different from other movement disciplines like dance and gymnastics. It is specific to the art of silent communication. Mario Diamond does a welcome service with this book, helping to promote the techniques and principles of our misunderstood and fragile art.

A warm and playful introduction to the world of mime. Much like its author, Mario Diamond, his book is full of character and charm. A welcome addition to the art of physical theatre to spark an interest in mime. Best read in silence.

- Jesse Dryden, Circus Director

Mario brings humanity to his work, from the stage to the classroom and everywhere in between. This book is a small window into his wondrous world of communication. A book that bridges language barriers, unifies us as humans, and teaches well beyond the art of mime.

- Deena Marcum Selko, MOTH Poetic Circus

Mario Diamond has written a tour de force on the art of mime. This book is eloquent and concise with very useful explanations of the details that go into silent physical communication - something everyone, everywhere could find useful... This is a must read, must use, book for anyone using physicality and gesture to communicate including dancers, acrobats, aerialists, jugglers, ice skaters, singers, actors, and politicians.

- Serenity Smith Forcion, New England Center for Circus Arts

Free eBook!

IF YOU ENJOYED *JUGGLING: or how to become a juggler*, you might be interested in *What Scientists Have to Say About Juggling*. A 15-page treatise on the current state of juggling research. This Amazon bestselling booklet outlines juggling and its effects on the practitioner's body and mind.

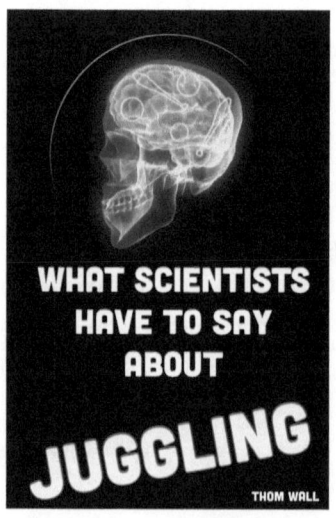

Now available as a free digital download!

http://thomwall.com/sciencebook

The nerdiest non-nerdy explanation of the current state of juggling research in the world. Super legit content, mixed with light touch of humor.

Craig Quat: www.quatprops.com

This ebook covers an incredible amount of research while keeping the information engaging and useful for a juggling practice. I have been either training, performing, or teaching juggling for about two decades, and I learned a ton! Whether you're just discovering an interest in juggling or you're far down the rabbit hole, read this today.

Jeremy Fein: www.feinmovement.com

This paper is in-depth, interesting, and informative. Thom has dug up some of the juiciest academic and scientific tidbits of our art to help legitimize and de-stigmatize the word "juggler." Time spent reading this book will not only deeply intrigue the casual reader but help facilitate the education potentials of teachers and hobbyists alike.

Benjamin Domask: www.benjamindomask.com

www.ingramcontent.com/pod-product-compliance
Lightning Source LLC
Chambersburg PA
CBHW060501080526
44584CB00015B/1512